THE MOUNT KAILASH TREK

A TREKKER'S AND VISITOR'S GUIDE

About the Authors

Siân Pritchard-Jones and Bob Gibbons met in 1983, on a trek from Kashmir to Ladakh. By then Bob had already driven an ancient Land Rover from England to Kathmandu in 1974 and led overland trips across Asia, Africa and South America as well as decrepit old tourist buses around India. He had also lived in Kathmandu as a trekking company manager. Before they met, Siân had worked in computer programming and systems analysis, but her heart had always been in the Himalayas, after a trip there on her way back from working in New Zealand.

Since they met they have been leading and organising treks in the Alps, Nepal, Algeria and Niger; they have hitched across Tibet, driven a busload of over-50s overland to Nepal, explored the Sahara and driven across Africa to Gabon. Some of this was real work, but luckily that 'proper job' has not materialised. A journey by slightly less ancient (only 21 years old) Land Rover from England to Cape Town, provided the basis for the fourth edition of the Bradt guide *Africa Overland*. In complete contrast Siân and Bob have since updated the Bradt guides to the Maldives and the Cape Verde islands.

However, they regularly return to their first love, Kathmandu and the Himalayas, where they work with Pilgrims Publishing in Kathmandu. For Pilgrims they have produced a cultural guide to the valley – *Kathmandu: Valley of the Green-Eyed Yellow Idol* – as well as new books on the monasteries of Ladakh (*Ladakh – Land of Magical Monasteries*) and a cultural, historical overview of the Guge kingdom (*Kailash and Guge – Land of the Tantric Mountain*).

Finally making it to Western Tibet was a wonderful experience, one to be shared with like-minded trekkers and travellers, for Kailash is surely the most mystical of all the fabulous Himalayan mountains.

THE MOUNT KAILASH TREK

A TREKKER'S AND VISITOR'S GUIDE

by

Siân Pritchard-Jones and Bob Gibbons

CICERONE

2 POLICE SQUARE, MILNTHORPE, CUMBRIA LA7 7PY

www.cicerone.co.uk

First edition 2007
ISBN-13: 978-1-85284-514-8

Photos: Siân Pritchard-Jones and Bob Gibbons

A catalogue record for this book is available from the British Library.

Acknowledgements

We are very grateful to Jonathan Williams of Cicerone Press for allowing us the pleasure of bringing the lands of Western Tibet, Kailash and the Guge kingdom to the attention of a wider audience through this book, and to Clare Crooke for her work on the book. Particular thanks must also go to Kev Reynolds, who over many years has inspired us with his books. Many thanks – *xie xie* – also to Philip Dorman, currently working in Shanghai, for his help with the Chinese phrases.

In Nepal we are indebted to Ravi Chandra and Amrit, who helped us to organise the trip to Kailash in spite of many bureaucratic obstacles. We are also grateful to Pasang Dawa for his information about the route from Simikot to Tibet, because the border was closed due to political instability in the region and we were unable to travel that way. Many thanks to Karna, Rajan, Sunil and Susan Sakya, Sohan Shrestha, Uttam Phuyal and all the staff at the Kathmandu Guest House, for making our stays so pleasant. Thanks to Rama and Pushpa Tiwari, Rhicha, Lala, Ashish, Sunil and all the staff at Pilgrims Book House in Kathmandu, where much of the cultural and historical text was researched. Thanks also to Tsering Dolkar Lama, Dilip Singh Kapoor, Tony Jones, Yogendra and Bindu Sakya, Janaki Man Shrestha, Bhandari's Photo Shop and ColorLink photo lab. In Tibet, thanks to our safe driver and guides.

Finally, thanks to our parents, Marianne and John, Beryl and Tony, who have generally supported us in our desires to seek out these uncomfortable, occasionally harrowing but immensely exciting destinations.

Front cover: Kailash south face and Nandi peak

CONTENTS

Advice to Readers

Readers are advised that while every effort is taken by the author to ensure the accuracy of this guidebook, changes can occur which may affect the contents. It is advisable to check locally on transport, accommodation, shops, etc, but even rights of way can be altered.

The publisher would welcome notes of any such changes.

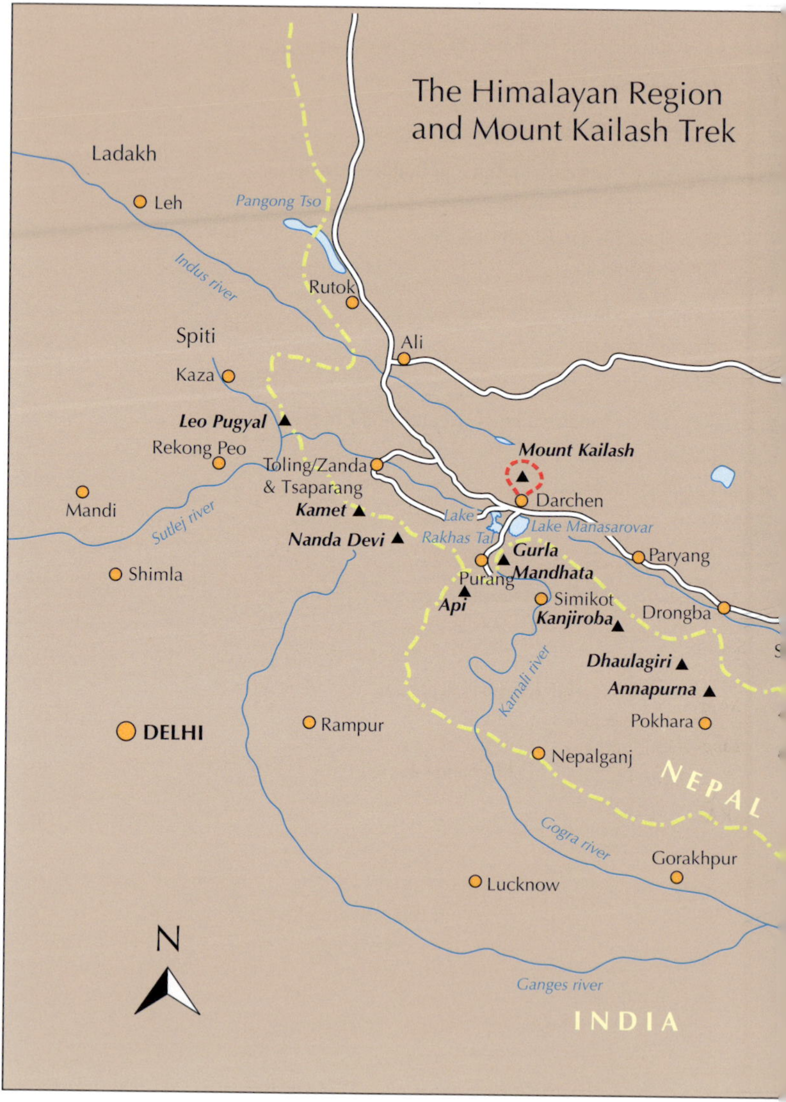

The Himalayan Region and Mount Kailash Trek
Ladakh
Leh
Pangong Tso
Indus river
Rutok
Ali
Spiti
Kaza
Leo Pugyal
Rekong Peo
Toling/Zanda & Tsaparang
Mandi
Sutlej river
Kamet
Nanda Devi
Mount Kailash
Darchen
Lake Rakhas Tal
Lake Manasarovar
Gurla Mandhata
Purang
Api
Paryang
Simikot
Kanjiroba
Drongba
Shimla
Dhaulagiri
Annapurna
Karnali river
Pokhara
DELHI
Rampur
Nepalganj
NEPAL
Gogra river
Gorakhpur
Lucknow
N
Ganges river
INDIA

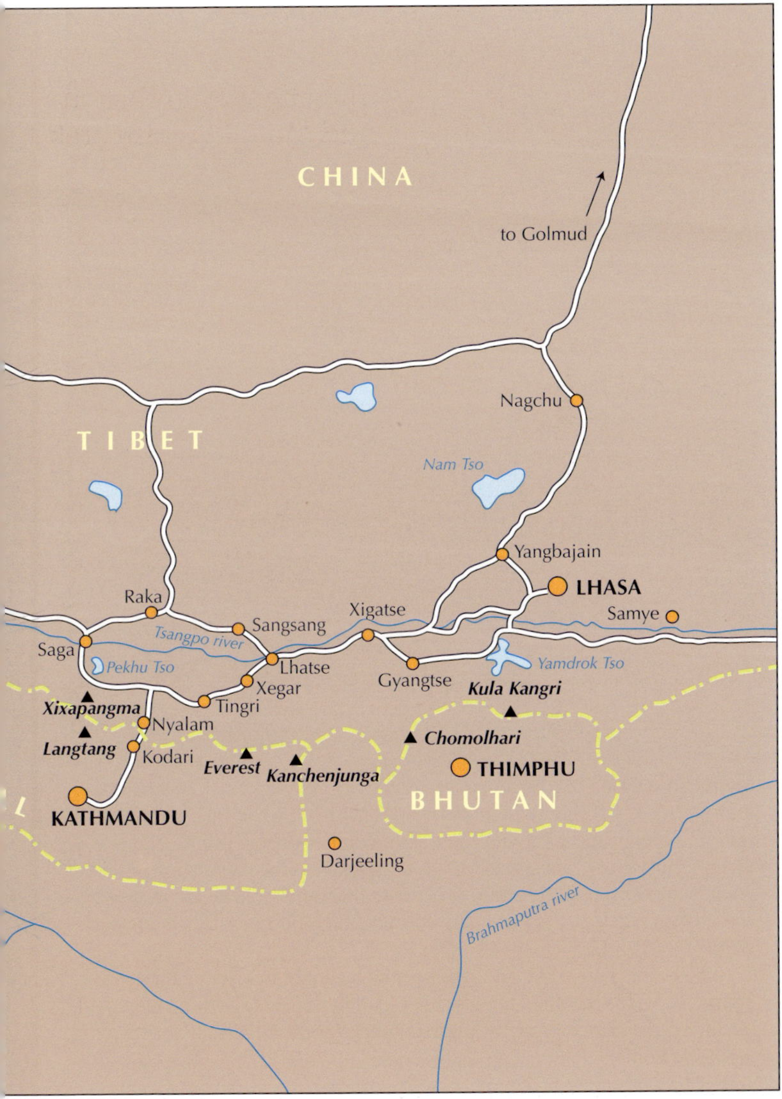
CHINA
to Golmud
TIBET
Nagchu
Nam Tso
Yangbajain
LHASA
Samye
Raka
Xigatse
Sangsang
Tsangpo river
Saga
Pekhu Tso
Lhatse
Gyangtse
Yamdrok Tso
Xegar
Tingri
Kula Kangri
Xixapangma
Nyalam
Chomolhari
Langtang
Kodari
Everest
Kanchenjunga
THIMPHU
BHUTAN
KATHMANDU
Darjeeling
Brahmaputra river

Map Key

road	devotional spot
ridge	monastery
national boundary	mountain peak
main route	campsite
alternative route	pass
river	town
lake	place of interest
glacier	viewpoint

PREFACE

Having spent many years working in Nepal and the Himalayas, and almost as many in the Alps, it was inevitable that one day we would make a trip to Kailash in Tibet. Perhaps the surprise is that it took so long! Pilgrims have been seeking the powers of Kailash as a spiritual centre for centuries, but apart from a few early missionaries, adventurers and explorers, it is only in more recent years that recreational trekkers and visitors have been admitted.

One of the classic walks of the world, some might consider the hike around Kailash's captivating circumference to be simply a challenging trek. For others, the sheer beauty of the Tibetan landscapes and the Himalayas will draw them in. The spiritual aspects of the peak will undoubtedly attract some visitors, those seeking inspiration and searching inwardly for renewal. Pilgrims do it in the hope of obtaining forgiveness for their sins. Whatever the reasons for coming here, all visitors will be challenged both physically and emotionally. All are sure to find inspiration for their souls while creating perspiration from their earthly bodies!

It is unlikely that most hikers will be interested in Kailash purely as a mountain to walk around in three or four days, particularly when getting there is an epic journey in itself. The peak has a special spiritual meaning for Hindus, Buddhists, Bonpo and Jains. Many of the rocks and surrounding peaks have a particular significance, knowledge of which will add immeasurably to a trekker's enjoyment of the Kailash circuit or *kora*. Glancing through this book will provide an excuse to stop for a minute or two to rest, as well as to savour the moment!

A brief overview of Tibet's history and its religious aspects is provided. Getting to Kailash is an adventure in itself, so we have included notes on the main places of interest along the access routes from Kathmandu, Simikot and Lhasa.

There is no way that this expedition to Kailash can be underrated in terms of objective dangers, such is the remoteness of the area. Because of this isolation and the difficulty of access, advance preparation is vital. A chapter is devoted to this, and includes sections dealing with health and altitude sickness.

Also, having travelled so far, it would be a great shame to miss out on exploring Tibet's 'secret Shangri-la' – the ancient kingdom of Guge and its incredible scenery. The lost cities of Toling and Tsaparang are simply stunning, with their indescribable citadels, monasteries, astonishing art, frescoes and statues.

We hope this easy-to-carry guide will be a useful companion in Tibet, on the trails to the most mysterious of mountains.

Siân and Bob

Red Hayagriva (Tamdrin) icon at Drongba monastery (Paryang to Saga)

INTRODUCTION

The power of such a mountain is so great and yet so subtle that, without compulsion, people are drawn to it from near and far, as if by the force of some invisible magnet; and they will undergo untold hardships and privations in their inexplicable urge to approach and to worship the centre of this sacred power.

The Way of the White Clouds Lama Anagarika Govinda

Hidden and isolated for centuries behind the nearly impenetrable barrier of the Himalayas is a mysterious and mythical mountain. Kailash has been variously called the centre of the universe, the navel of the earth, a resting place for the Gods and 'the precious snow mountain'; for more than a thousand years it has been a central pilgrimage site for some of the world's major religions.

Kailash is 6714m (22,028ft) high and lies just northwest of the western Nepal, Indian and Tibetan border. It is sacred to Hindus because Shiva, the god of destruction, sits here. Buddhists revere it as Kang Rinpoche, 'precious jewel of the snows', like a vast *chorten*, a pyramid of nature that can cleanse the sins of a lifetime. For the Bonpo, the first religious people of Tibet, it is Yungdrung Gutse or 'the nine-storied swastika mountain'. And finally, for the Jain pilgrims from India, it is the sacred peak of Asthapada, where the first Jain prophet gained enlightenment.

For the western visitor, Kailash is a mountain that equates to adventure; one of the wonders of the world, a landmark of inspirational beauty, a place to seek spiritual peace. It is a mountain that captures the imagination and breathes sheer excitement into the soul. A visit to Kailash will take one's breath away in many ways. A circuit of its mighty parapets is not to be lightly entertained. Kailash is, for many people, the spiritual centre of the universe, and for a few short days it will enthral and capture even the most atheistic of souls.

Tibet is a magical place. Today it is blessed with resurgent monasteries, myriad spectacular mountains and some fantastic hidden gems. The road to Kailash is studded with these jewels; stupendous scenery, clear luminescent light, crumbling history and vast rolling plains. Tibet is a harsh land with quaint villages and large yak herds set in a timeless landscape. Its curious, lively and friendly people and its ancient religion make it a very special place.

Kailash from the south

With this comprehensive guide a door will open into the enchanting world of the Kailash region. On a journey around the sacred peak, the trekker will be in awe of its eerie, surreal canyons, marvel at the striking and strange contorted rock formations and, without doubt, will huff and puff to the highest point, the Drolma La, the pass of the goddess Tara. At the sacred lake pilgrims seek penance in its icy waters, and lower down are welcomed by nomad tents serving warming drinks. The sheer wonder and variety of the walk around Kailash make it one of the world's greatest treks.

But there is one further inspirational destination that we include in this book. No journey or trek to the region would be complete without a visit to the lost kingdom of Guge. Where the northern slopes of the Indian Himalayas hide the headwaters of the Sutlej river, in a vast maze of crazily eroded sandstone towers, are the ethereal fortress ruins of Tsaparang, the former capital of Guge. This is Tibet's greatest treasurehouse of Buddhist art and paintings, a fairytale location not to be missed, a place so unique that its fame will surely spread.

The aim of this guide is to inspire adventure-seeking trekkers to go beyond the familiar, to break free and explore the last bastions of mystery on the roof of the world. The raw power of nature's grandeur is to be observed right here in Tibet, the land of the snows.

GEOGRAPHY

Who can put into words a landscape that breathes this immensity?—where vast blue lakes, set in emerald-green pastures and golden foothills, are seen against a distant range of snow mountains, in the centre of which rises the dazzling dome of Kailash, the 'Jewel of the Snows', as the Tibetans call the holy mountain.

The Way of the White Clouds Lama Anagarika Govinda

TIBETAN LANDSCAPES

The Tibetan plateau and the neighbouring state of Xinjiang comprise almost half of modern China. The autonomous region of Tibet lies north of the Himalayas, east of Indian Ladakh and west of China's great river systems. To the north are the deserts of Xinjiang and to the northeast is the region of Qinghai. Kailash is located in the western region of Tibet known as Ngari, roughly 900km west of Lhasa, and over 1000km southeast of Kashgar in Xinjiang province. The nearest large settlement is Ali, also known as Senge Tsangpo (Tibetan) and Shiquanhe (Chinese). Most of the plateau is a mix of rugged mountain ranges interspersed with rolling plains and lakes.

Kailash does not form part of the main Himalayan chain, whose crest delineates the international border between Tibet, India and Nepal. Its dominant, almost isolated summit is

Kailash from the plains south of Darchen (Lake Manasarovar to Darchen)

to be found in the range north of the main Himalayan arc, known as the Kangtise range. It is this mountain range that is the true watershed of the Tibetan plateau. From the base of these peaks emanate four of the main rivers of Asia. Within less than a hundred miles of Kailash are the headwaters of the Indus, the Tsangpo, the Sutlej and the Karnali.

According to Tibetan mythology, these rivers, which are the lifeblood of India, Pakistan, Bangladesh and Tibet, issue from the mouths of different animals. The Indus is the lion's mouth river, which issues to the north; its Tibetan name is Senge Khambab. The Tsangpo, which becomes the Brahmaputra in India, is the horse's mouth river and heads east; it is called the Tamchok Khambab. The Mapchu Khambab emanates from the peacock's mouth and is the river of the south; this is the Karnali of Nepal, which eventually joins the Ganges. The Langchan Khambab rises from the mouth of an elephant and heads west, becoming the Sutlej of the Punjab. Buddhists see these rivers, together with Kailash, as a gigantic mandala, a geometric vision that represents a perfect state of peace.

Much of modern western Tibet is within a region known in ancient times as the land of Shangshung; a land said by many to be perhaps the mythical location of Shangri-La. The kingdom of Guge, in the upper basins of the Sutlej river, was also within ancient Shangshung, 200km

Indian Himalayas, including Kamet, high above Toling (Toling to Darchen)

A BON LEGEND ABOUT THE ORIGINS OF TIBET

According to ancient legends of Tibet, the land was under the sea in primordial times. Around this vast sea, plants began to grow and wild animals roamed along the shores. One day a five-headed dragon came from the sea and began to endanger life along the shores. In order to stop this destruction, five female divinities came from a cloud of many colours and vanquished the dragon. After the dragon was slain, they remained to protect the animals and plants by becoming five mountain peaks that grew to become the Himalayas.

west of Kailash. The landscape of this region is a remarkable sight, characterised by deeply eroded sandstone and mud deposits. Great pinnacles, spires and gullies have been cut out of the ancient soft layers. Mud castles, fortresses and troglodyte caves blend into the natural features to form a bewitching and unworldly scene.

The historical boundaries of the Guge kingdom extended across the main Himalayan divide into India and the region northeast of modern-day Shimla. The Sutlej river cuts through the mountains here and descends through the regions of Spiti and Kinnaur.

From the abundant fossil records in Tibet and Nepal, it is estimated that a sea existed here about 100 million years ago. Sometime in the following 50 million years, India began to collide with Tibet through a process known as plate tectonics. These plates within the earth's crust create mountains where they collide. Thus the Himalayan uplift began and the first mountains were formed. These ranges are now the Kangtise and the Nyenchenyangla, known as the Transhimalaya, on the southern edge of the Tibetan plateau, and the Kunlun, which forms its northern rim. It is likely that Kailash has existed for 50 million years. Some 40 to 45 million years ago, the Indian plate continued its northward march, forcing the plateau upwards, and about 20 million years ago, the main Himalayan chain was formed. The plateau region has risen even further over the last two million years, as have the Himalayas.

FLORA AND FAUNA

Plants

The Tibetan plateau is not a pure desert, although it is largely made up of rolling plains cut by rivers, indented with lakes and dissected by dry mountain ranges. Much of the region is treeless, but grasses do survive and are luxuriant during the summer rains. Juniper and berberis bushes struggle to exist in sheltered spots.

Poplar trees and willow, although rare, also exist, for example in sheltered spots like Toling.

Birds

The arid plateau region has limited bird life but the lake areas attract more species. Bar-headed geese and Brahminy ducks are found on Lake Manasarovar and other lakes. One would be lucky to see Himalayan vultures though. The Chakor is another larger bird found in the region. Siberian cranes migrate south across Tibet into Mustang and the Kali Gandaki valley of the Annapurnas in Nepal in season.

Animals

Wild animals are not plentiful in number or variety because of the harsh environment.

The animal perhaps most commonly associated with Tibet is the yak. Although in isolated areas wild yaks do still roam the more remote valleys, most of the yak herds seen are domesticated. As well as making the infamous butter tea, yak milk is used by nomads to produce cheese and yoghurt. A *dzo* is a commonly seen cross between a yak and a cow. Nomads have flocks of domesticated sheep and goats, as well as their yaks.

You are likely to see herds of wild ass, the *khyang*. These skittish animals carry their heads proudly and have a long black line stretching from their heads to their tails. They are similar to donkeys but reddish brown on top and white or grey underneath. They are not domesticated.

Rabbits and small marmot-like mammals called *chiwa* scurry about.

Group of Khyang near Paryang, with the Himalayas behind (Saga to Paryang)

An unusual gerbil-like rodent found here is called the *abra*. It lives in burrows, often in small colonies.

Mountain deer, antelope and gazelle are fleet of foot and can travel at high speed, sometimes even as fast as a 4x4 car on the rough Tibetan roads. Gazelle – small, agile and shy – are sometimes seen across the plains. The Hodgson antelope is another grazing beast, with long horns and white underside. You might also see *markor* – wild goats – sometimes as large as a stag, with a reddish brown colour, but they are rare. Another wild goat, the light brown *shyin*, is also rare and more commonly found in Ladakh. There are brown bears in much lower forests, but not around Kailash. Blue sheep (*bharal*), fox and snow wolves also live in the region. Wolves, although rarely seen, are a menace to antelope and the herds of the nomadic Drokpa people across the plateau.

The snow leopard is a highly elusive animal, rarely encountered and hardly ever photographed. Hunting in the dawn or twilight hours, they are extremely wary and unlikely to show themselves to casual visitors. Television crews with big budgets have waited many years to capture images of these beautiful creatures.

As for the yeti, it remains even more elusive than the snow leopard. If you see one, let us know!

CLIMATE

To see the greatness of a mountain, one must keep one's distance, to understand its form, one must move around it; to experience its moods, one must see it at sunrise and sunset, at noon and at midnight, in sun and in rain, in snow and in storm, in summer and in winter and in all the other seasons.

The Way of the White Clouds Lama Anagarika Govinda

The climate of Tibet is not as unpleasant as one might expect. There are four main seasons, but the predominant feature of the climate is the influence of the high altitude. With much of the country lying at over 4000m, the most noticeable effect is the difference felt between days that are sunny, those that are cloudy and those where wind is prevalent. It should be noted that wind, in particular, will seriously aggravate any existing cold weather and trekkers should plan for such extreme conditions. The vastness of the country introduces significant local variations in weather patterns.

The Changtang plains in the far north of Tibet have a more markedly continental climate, with extremely cold temperatures. The eastern dissected Tibetan region is influenced by the milder climate of the adjacent Sichuan province. This brings wetter

North of Saga (Saga to Paryang)

weather and some amelioration of temperatures. Western Tibet comes under the influence of the Central Asian weather patterns, again bringing potentially bitter temperatures in winter. The south has a climate influenced by the Himalayan mountains.

The warmest time of year is the summer, when monsoon rains from India drift across the Himalayas. Clouds are not uncommon during this period, but temperatures are moderate. September and October mark the autumnal season, when temperatures begin to fall and nights become frosty. Days are generally clear after mid-September and into October; one can then expect clear, stable weather. That said, the chance of snowstorms in October has recently increased, although they rarely last more than three days. They often originate in the Bay of Bengal and affect Nepal at the same time. A very bad storm occurred in mid-October 2005 and tragically wiped out a French expedition on the Nepalese side of the mountains. Less severe storms have also become an erratic feature.

Winters are predominantly dry but temperatures range from very cold to bitterly cold, with the northern zones experiencing temperatures below -30°C. Snow in winter either comes from Mongolia and the north, or Central Asia in the west. Winter generally lasts from mid-November until well into March. Lhasa does not experience a lot of snowfall. Average temperatures in Lhasa range from -10°C in winter to 24°C in early summer.

Spring arrives any time in April, as temperatures rise. The snow melts and roads are often washed out. The period through May is generally quite conducive to trekking, but strong winds can be a problem. In fact, wind at any time of year will bring chill factors that seriously erode personal comfort. During cloud-free days the heat of the sun is surprisingly hot, even on the coldest winter day. Although pleasant, this is tempered by the dangers of sunburn on pale western faces. When clouds obscure this warming sunlight, the temperature plummets.

Temperature and weather statistics for Western Tibet are not currently available. The following chart is for Lhasa and may be of use in estimating conditions for the Kailash region. Assume that temperatures are colder and that there is a little less rainfall.

Typical temperatures

Month	Av Sunlight Hours	Temp Av. Min.	Temp Av. Max.	Temp Record Min.	Temp Record Max.	Relative Humidity	Av. Precip.mm.	Wet days > 0.25mm
Jan	6	-10	7	-16	16	71	0	0
Feb	6	-7	9	-15	22	71	13	0.4
March	8	-2	12	-10	21	72	8	1
April	6	1	16	-8	24	67	5	0.4
May	5	5	19	-3	26	59	25	3
June	2	9	24	2	32	64	64	8
July	2	9	23	2	29	71	122	13
Aug	3	9	22	3	27	72	89	10
Sept	5	7	21	0	26	71	66	7
Oct	10	1	17	-8	23	64	13	2
Nov	10	-5	13	-12	21	71	3	0.1
Dec	9	-9	9	-15	16	71	0	0

Temperature chart taken from the BBC weather website (www.bbc.co.uk/weather), showing available information for Lhasa.

No precise figures are available for the Kailash region. However, the weather conditions are colder and generally more severe, while the conditions can be stunning in the sunshine.

The specific effects of the climate on trekkers are discussed in 'Predeparture preparation' below.

Shegar, the old Dzong and monastery village

TIBETAN CULTURE

BRIEF HISTORY OF THE TIBET REGION

The history of Tibet is a complex blend of legend, historical fact and religious development. All these themes are intricately woven into its resilient culture and traditions.

According to legend, the mythical ancestors of Tibet are the Bon mountain deity and the Buddhist monkey. These two unlikely characters supposedly fell in love. Their children eventually turned into humans and they learnt how to grow crops.

There are thought to have been four original tribes of Tibet: the Dong, Tong, Se and Mu. However, the earliest records are from the first established inhabitants, the Bonpo people. The Bonpo had a unique religion, known as Bon. Their ancestral homeland centred on Khyunglung, just to the southwest of Kailash, in the land called Shangshung. Ancient texts suggest that there were perhaps 32 early rulers, collectively referred to as the Pugyel kings.

These little-known Pugyel kings predated the well-chronicled Yarlung dynasty, whose settlements in central Tibet were loosely federated from the sixth century. The unification of Tibet took place in the mid-seventh century under Namri Srongtsen. In 642AD, his son, Srongtsen Gampo (609–650AD), became king. He was fascinated by stories of a religion to the south. He married the Nepalese Princess Bhrikuti Devi and the Chinese Princess Wengchen, both of whom were devout Buddhists, and made Buddhism the state religion. However, much of Tibet continued neither to fully accept nor completely reject the new religion.

King Trisong Detsen came to the throne in the mid-eighth century, bringing a renewed interest in Buddhism. Santarakshita, an Indian Buddhist teacher, was enlisted to enlighten his subjects. Trisong Detsen also invited another Tantric master, Padma Sambhava, to come from India to help promote the religion. Padma Sambhava was the founder of the first Buddhist sect, the Nyingma-pa; he is known as Guru Rinpoche in Tibet. All across Tibet there are caves and meditation sites that are closely associated with Guru Rinpoche. King Trisong Detsen died in 797AD.

Another king, Ralpachen, also aided the cause of Buddhist development and gave the country some of its finest scriptures, translated from Indian Sanskrit. However, he also faced renewed challenges from the Bon. In 838AD his brother, Langdarma, assassinated him. Langdarma was a staunch adherent to Bon practices and he re-established Bon. Four years later he

A LEGEND OF LANGDARMA

During the Cham festivities, which involved masked dancers, a monk called Palgyi Dorje took part dressed in a black cloak with a white lining. Before arriving he covered his white horse in charcoal, to make it black. During the festivities he killed the Bon King Langdarma with his arrow, then escaped on his horse. To avoid detection he rushed into a river, where his black horse became white and he turned his cloak inside out.

was murdered by a Buddhist monk. There was little coherent government after this assassination and Tibet descended into disorder.

In the 10th century, a revival of Buddhism in Tibet began in the western region under the Guge king, Kor De, more commonly known as Lama Yeshe O. His famous translator, Rinchen Zangpo (958–1055), is credited with establishing 108 monasteries, including Toling and Tsaparang in Tibet, and Tabo, Nako and Alchi in India. Yeshe O also invited another Indian Buddhist master, Atisha (982–1054), to come to Tibet. Atisha spent three years in Toling monastery and, through his great knowledge of Buddhism and his compassionate teachings, succeeded in reviving Buddhism. He founded the Kadam-pa sect. Buddhism spread from western Tibet to encompass the whole country.

Following in Atisha's footsteps, Marpa founded the Kagyu-pa sect, which emphasises both physical and mental methods of meditation. Milarepa (1040–1123) was his disciple. He became famous in Tibet for his solitary meditation in numerous caves that are now revered on different parts of the plateau. The Kagyu-pa spread throughout the country, but remained strong in the Kailash region. Power in Tibet remained in the central regions in the Kyi Chu valley of Lhasa.

The Tang and Song dynasties of China had little or no contact with Tibet, so, with little outside interference, Tibetan Buddhism diversified. In 1073, Konchok Gyalpo and his son Kunga Nyingpo founded a monastery at Sakya, near modern-day Lhatse. Systematic study of the Buddhist scriptures was emphasised by this new sect, the Sakya-pa.

In the 13th century, the conquering hordes of Genghis Khan shattered the existing status quo across the whole of China, Tibet and Mongolia. However, Tibet escaped most of the marauding armies' devastating raids, because one of the Mongol warlords, Godan Khan, embraced the Sakya-pa Buddhist ideals, making it the dominant ruling sect until 1326. With the fall of the Mongolian court, the region reverted to its former independent nations. The Sakya-pa was dominant for around a hundred years. By the

River Sutlej near Toling (Lake Manasarovar to Toling)

mid-14th century there were effectively four major Buddhist sects in Tibet: Nyingma-pa, Kadam-pa, Kagyu-pa and Sakya-pa.

The next great reformer of Buddhism, Tsong Khapa, was born in 1357. After study of the different branches, he initiated reforms of the Kadam-pa teachings (of Atisha) to create the Gelug-pa, the Yellow Hat sect. Tsong Khapa established the great monastery of Ganden (New Kadam-pa), as well as Sera and Drepung just outside Lhasa. The Yellow Hats adopted the ideas of reincarnation and also initiated the position of Dalai Lama, meaning 'Ocean of Wisdom'.

The first three Dalai Lamas had little influence and the fourth Dalai Lama died in mysterious circumstances. The next incarnate was Ngawang Gyatso, who became known as the Great Fifth. He lived from 1617 to 1682. With the aid of Mongolian patronage, the fifth reincarnate became the effective holder of power in Tibet. He held the positions of both head of state and spiritual leader. In the west a brief war between Ladakh and Tibet ended in 1665, with the Guge kingdom diminished by the loss of the western regions of Kinnaur and Spiti to Ladakh.

Successive Dalai Lamas were found as children, often after elaborate rituals to locate and ascertain prospective candidates' true credentials as reincarnates. The sixth Dalai Lama was a wayward individual, more interested in women than study! Most others never reached maturity to take power, often being poisoned or dying young in mysterious circumstances. Because of this, power was retained by a series of regents. The long transition times between Dalai Lamas allowed for greater interference from outside.

China and, to a degree, Mongolia, were both instrumental in the power struggles within Tibet. In 1717 the Dzungur Mongolians captured Lhasa; the town was not relieved until 1720, when the Chinese ousted the interlopers. Since then, China has made claims on Tibet. Again in 1792, following a Gurkha invasion from Nepal, it was the Chinese army that repelled the invaders. Afterwards the Manchurian dynasty (from the far northeast) held the reins of power in China. Tibet was effectively sealed off from the outside world after 1860 and it remained so until 1985, when the first independent travellers were allowed to enter this mysterious land. However, during this time a few intrepid explorers did still travel in Tibet clandestinely, including the Indian Pundits (spies) sent by the British, who helped to map Tibet secretly.

Far to the west, beyond the tentacles of Lhasa, other significant events took place in Guge. The kingdom's power lasted for over 600 years until 1630, when it was overthrown

Sunrise on the Potala, Lhasa

because of religious differences. The Portuguese Jesuit missionary, Antonio de Andrade, entered Tsaparang from the Mana pass north of the Garhwal peaks of India in August 1624. He left but later returned, and in April 1626 a church was built, with the support of the king. However, in 1630 the Lamas of Tsaparang, fearing pollution from the new religion, connived with the neighbouring Ladakhis to overthrow the Guge monarch. The kingdom never recovered from this and went into decline.

In the late 19th century, the quest for control of Central Asia became known as the Great Game, with Russia, China and British India vying for land and influence. The British were more concerned with trade than anything else. In 1774 the Bogle mission to Tibet was essentially one to secure British and Bhutanese peace and an end to raids across the borders. The further missions of Turner and Manning followed; Manning did reach Lhasa. The now infamous march to Lhasa of Sir Francis Younghusband's mission in 1903–4 was ostensibly due to trade and the fear of a further increase in Russian influence in Tibet. It did little to foster good relations and ended ignominiously, with many Tibetans dead and no formal agreements, the 13th Dalai Lama (1876–1933) having fled to Mongolia.

The Manchurians invaded Tibet in 1910, forcing the Dalai Lama to flee to British India. He became a much stronger character after this. When the Manchu dynasty collapsed a year later, he returned and became the effective ruler of Tibet. He attempted to introduce a number of modernising ideas, but was to some degree thwarted by intransigent conservative powers from within the monastic community. This was a period of ever-closer ties between British India and Tibet, when expeditions to climb Mount Everest were permitted on the north side. It was on the third expedition, in 1924, that George Mallory and Andrew Irvine disappeared into the clouds and died, perhaps having reached the summit, perhaps not. The death of the 13th incarnate brought little outward change and the regents pursued the same policies, keeping Tibet isolated and inward-looking.

The 14th Dalai Lama, Tenzin Gyatso, the current incumbent, was found in 1940. He came from the far northeast and was 'discovered' by the Reting Rinpoche, who later fell from favour. In 1950, following the victory of Mao Tse Tung over Chiang Kai Chek's nationalists, Chinese forces entered Tibet. The young Dalai Lama was enthroned at the age of 15. He made one visit to Peking and met Mao. He remained in Lhasa until 1959 and then went into exile in India, where he remains to this day.

Since 1959, Tibet has been modernising, with astonishingly rapid changes taking place after 1985. The most profound effects of this rush for modernity have been in Lhasa. At the time of our early visits to Tibet in

Siling village, local people (Xixapangma Trekking Routes)

1985–6, Lhasa was a small town, with muddy streets and a charming mediaeval atmosphere. Construction on a grand scale has radically changed it into a modern city, but there remains an air of mystery because of the incredible Potala Palace which still dominates the skyline.

EARLY FOREIGN VISITORS TO KAILASH

Rumours of a sacred mountain beyond the Himalayas emerged sporadically, but little was known of Kailash itself or its position on a map. In 1624 the Portuguese Jesuit missionary Antonio de Andrade entered Tibet, but he did not venture much beyond the Guge kingdom, west of the mountain. The first European visitors to the mountain were probably Ippolito Desideri and Manuel Freyra, also both Jesuit missionaries. They crossed western Tibet in 1715. Freyra returned to India, while Desideri continued east to Lhasa, where he arrived in 1716.

In 1812 a vet called William Moorcroft became the first English visitor. Having crossed the Himalayas from India, he set eyes on both Lake Manasarovar and Kailash. He did not circle the mountain, but merely remarked on its grandeur. He also noted that Darchen comprised only four houses. Moorcroft returned to India by way of Tirthapuri and Khyunglung along the Sutlej. Henry Strachey, another English pioneer, visited in 1846.

At the turn of the century, Ekai Kawaguchi, a celebrated Japanese explorer, spent three years in Tibet disguised as a monk, between 1897 and 1903. He actually walked the Kailash Kora, one of the first foreign visitors to do so. Another famous visitor to the region was the Swedish explorer Sven Hedin, who passed through in 1907 during one of his celebrated journeys to Tibet and Central Asia.

Today Kailash is more accessible than ever before. Its enduring fame is assured, but the pristine environment in which it stands today may not last as long.

RELIGIOUS ASPECTS OF KAILASH

Holy places never had any beginning. They have been holy from the time they were discovered, strongly alive because of the invisible presences breathing through them. Man is amazed or fearful as he feels the vibrations of invisible power in the air...

Tibet: The Land of Snows
Giuseppe Tucci

The near-perfect conical summit of Kailash is a spectacular sight from any angle, and to each side is attributed a precious jewel. The south is commonly called the sapphire face, and the east is the crystal face. The west face is ruby and the north is gold, a colour it adopts at sunset or sunrise. The striking geography of the mountain is inspirational, but it is its holy significance that attracts most visitors.

For the **Hindu** pilgrim, Kailash is the home of the God of Destruction, Shiva, and his consort, Parvati. It is considered to be the centre of the universe, the mythical Mount Meru, and the navel of the world. The stars, sun and moon supposedly revolve around the peak. Hindus also believe that an invisible strand of the river Ganges flows from the mountain to India.

The Shiva Purana, an Indian scripture, says: 'There is no sin in the world which cannot be destroyed by circumambulation. Hence one should dispel all sins by circumambulation alone.' It is this holy text that inspires so many Indian visitors to undertake the dangerous and difficult pilgrimage to Kailash. The Hindus call the Kora circle route the **Parikrama.** Most come

A LEGEND OF SHIVA AT KAILASH

While Shiva was in lonely meditation, the lower gods realised that, unless he had a son, the demons would inherit the earth. They sent Parvati, a beautiful daughter of the Himalayas, to seduce Shiva, but she sat in meditation for thousands of years before gaining his attention. Then Kama, the god of love, shot an arrow at Shiva, but Shiva saw it and burned him to ashes with his flaming eye. Too late though, for the arrow hit him; he spied Parvati and fell in love. Their son Karttikeya was born of this love, to save the world from evil.

Snow Lion

Avalokiteshvara Bodhisattva image

on foot from Nainital by way of the Lipu Lekh pass, just west of the Nepal border. For the Hindu, Kailash abounds in legends and none is more famous than the legend of the meeting of Shiva and Parvati.

For the first religious people of Tibet, the **Bonpo**, Kailash is known as Yungdrung Gutse, often translated as 'the nine-storey swastika mountain'. It lies close to the centre of the ancient Bon territory known as Shangshung. The mountain is the dwelling place of Ku Lha Gekho, a Bon protective deity and also the place where the founder of the Bon, Tonpa Shenrab, descended to earth from heaven. The Bon divide the mountain into three zones that are ruled by different deities. These are the zone above the peak, the mountain itself and the zone below the earthly vision of Kailash.

Bon pilgrims follow the Kora path in an anticlockwise direction, making them easily recognisable. For the Bon the Drolma La pass poses an even more substantial obstacle, for it is harder to climb from east to west. The sorrowful ruins of an ancient Bon monastery are found just east of Kailash, below a snowy peak called Bon Ri.

Buddhists call Kailash 'Kang Rinpoche', the 'snows of the precious jewel'. Buddhist pilgrims follow the conventional direction, clockwise, around the Kailash Kora. Demchok is their guardian deity of the peak; he is often depicted in a Tantric pose with his consort, Dorje Phagmo. She resides on the snowy turret-like spire of Tijung, just west of Kailash. Together they create compassion and wisdom for enlightenment.

A BON LEGEND OF YARLHA SHAMPO

Yarlha Shampo is a sacred mountain of the Bon north of Bhutan. Yarlha Shampo is also a Bon deity who once took the form of a white yak in a magical contest with the Buddhist sage and Tantric, Guru Rinpoche. Yarlha Shampo lost the contest when Guru Rinpoche covered him with his magic cloak. And, so it is said, the Bon deity was converted to Buddhism!

Monk and prayer wheel (Kailash Kora trek, Stage 2)

The Buddhist hermit sage, Milarepa, wrote of Kailash: 'This is a place in the Himalayas, where one can barter the vortex of life for endless bliss.' Buddhists believe that the walk around the mountain brings enlightenment, freedom from earthly sorrows and desires. By crossing the Drolma La pass, they also divest themselves of their burdens of previous sin. Many pilgrims prostrate themselves around the mountain and, having accomplished 13 circuits of the Kora, they are eligible to undertake the Inner Kora.

The Tantric magician Guru Rinpoche, who helped introduce Buddhist practices to Tibet from India, meditated in the Kailash region. In one Tibetan legend Kailash is a black mountain with a nine-storey crystal temple on the summit.

Finally, Kailash is known by the **Jains** as Asthapada. The peak is where the first Jain prophet, Adinath Rasbhanatha, gained enlightenment. Jains believe, like Hindus and Buddhists, in karmic interactions, the idea that any action will produce a reaction. They contend that all living things have an internal soul that never dies. However, to reach enlightenment (*nirvana*), one must free the soul. Jains also divide the world into three levels. The upper world is for the gods, the middle world is the place of all living things and the lower world is the place of demons.

Parsva and Mahavira, two earthly figures from India revered by Jains, are credited with introducing the Jain ideals. Mahavira, like the Buddha, renounced all comforts and pleasures to become a roaming soul. He meditated and wandered without clothing for 12 years. After this time he reached a state of great knowledge. His ascetic ways and charismatic words encouraged thousands to follow his path.

A casual visitor may be hard pressed to differentiate between Buddhist, Hindu and Jain pilgrims on the Kora, but the Jain pilgrims often carry a bag containing prayer beads.

A BUDDHIST LEGEND OF KAILASH

The black lord, guardian of Kailash, became angry that too many pilgrims were visiting the holy 'crystal stupa' on the summit after their *kora* walk. He decided to banish the mountain to the serpent world to avoid further commotion. When Buddha heard about this, he went to the mountain at once with five hundred disciples. To prevent the black lord from absconding with Kailash, they secured the mountain using Buddha's footprints. Later they cast snow on to the summit, to prevent pilgrims treading on the holy summit ever again.

A LEGEND OF THE JAINS

Adinath Rasbhanatha was born in Ayodhya in Uttar Pradesh, a town that remains a place of holy pilgrimage for Hindus, Jains and Muslims today. He took two wives and was blessed with a son called Bharata. Rasbha realised that all life is transitory, so he began preaching. After thousands of years he finally retired to Asthapada, taking with him ten thousand monks. After six and a half days of fasting, he passed into enlightenment and was cremated by the gods. Later his son, Bharata, erected a mythical temple to Rasbhanatha on Asthapada (Kailash).

TIBETAN RELIGIONS

Bonpo

The earliest inhabitants of Tibet, the Bonpo, worshipped natural phenomena, like the heavens and mountain spirits, as well as natural powers such as rivers, thunder and trees. This also involved elements of black magic, sorcery and demon worship. The founder of the Bon was Tonpa Shenrab Miwoche, who is said in legends to have descended from heaven to earth by way of Kailash. The Bon seek the eternal truth and reality of life, and in this they are closely aligned with Buddhism.

Other sources suggest that the Bon came not from Tibet but from Olmolungring, a legendary place in Tazik, possibly once in the land of the Tajik people of Central Asia. Tazik is a name that appears in Bon literature. Less than 100km southwest of Kailash lie the ruins of Khyunglung Ngulkhar – the silver castle of the Khyung bird. This place is believed to be the spiritual, ancestral home of the Bon and the centre of Shangshung. Not far from Tirthapuri is the Gurugyam cave monastery, which clings to the side of a sheer cliff; this is also thought to have originally belonged to the Bon.

The first known Bon monastery was founded in 1072 at Yeru Wensakha, which is just east of Xigatse, along the river Tsangpo. It has since fallen into ruin, but other Bon monasteries exist today near here at Menri, Yungdrung Ling and Tradang. Closer to Nepal, en route to Kailash near Mount Xixapangma, is lake Pekhu Tso, which has a Bon monastery. Pelha Puk is located on the isolated east side of the lake. A Bon monastery is also located in the Tibetan Kyirong valley between Langtang and Ganesh Himal some 100km north of Kathmandu. Another major pilgrimage peak is Bonri in southeastern Tibet, close to Namche Barwa, where the Tsangpo river cuts into deep gorges before dropping into India as the Brahmaputra.

The ancient Bon believed that all life started from eggs. Bon incorporates many animal-headed demons

Bon masked dancers at Triten Norbutse monastery in Kathmandu

and deities as its protectors. The white yak is particularly revered. Many facets and features of Tibetan Buddhism originate from the Bon. In the masked Cham dances that are staged by the Bon, animal and the protector Khyung-bird heads are used. The Khyung bird is very reminiscent of the Hindu god, Garuda. The Bon's sacred symbol, the Yungdrung, is very similar to the Tantric Buddhists' *dorje*, the thunderbolt sceptre. The Bon also use the swastika sign, but theirs usually, although not always, turns to the left. The use of prayer flags, the concept of the oracles or trance doctors and many of their deities have been incorporated into Buddhist ideas.

A BON LEGEND ABOUT THE ORIGINS OF LIFE

The ancient Bon believed that all life began from a single egg, from which hatched Sipai Sangpo Bumtri and the primordial mother, Sipai Gyalmo. She had many relationships, producing three sets of nine eggs. All the eggs hatched but one, producing only daughters. The 27th egg fell into the hands of a demon king and, with his help, the last egg hatched to produce the Queen of the Underworld.

In 1977 the Tibetan government-in-exile in Dharamsala recognised and accepted the Bon as a fifth Tibetan sect. The spiritual head of the Bon is known as Trizin. New Menri monastery at Dolanji near Shimla in Himachal Pradesh is the home of the exiled Bon community in India. Triten Norbutse monastery is their spiritual home in Kathmandu. Anyone interested in Bon should make a point of visiting this monastic complex close to Swayambhunath, such is the rarity of any active Bon culture today.

Buddhism

Although Buddhism is considered to be a religion, it can also be viewed as a philosophy, a direction for living, a search for true self and purpose, aiming towards inner peace of mind and cessation of worldly suffering. Reincarnation is a central theme of Tibetan Buddhism; the essence of the soul is developed through rebirth in successive lives until a state of perfect enlightenment is attained.

Prince Gautama Siddhartha, who became the earthly Buddha, was born the son of a Hindu king near present-day Lumbini in southern Nepal. His early life was one of luxury. Not until his 29th year did he become aware of his own sheltered existence and indolence. Tormented by his empty, materialistic life, he left his wife and newborn son to become an ascetic. Though he wandered far and wide, listening to sages, wise men and Brahmin priests, he found no solace.

After much thoughtful meditation, he chose to follow a pathway of

Guru Rinpoche figure at Drongba monastery (Paryang to Saga)

Guardian deity at Drongba monastery (Paryang to Saga)

acceptance. He preached a lifestyle following a middle way that acknowledges all worldly suffering, a way that could lead to a state of peace and enlightenment. Thus began Buddhism, in approximately 550BC. The Buddha is still considered by Hindus to be an incarnation of their god Vishnu.

Buddhism later split amicably and without conflict into two branches, Hinayana and Mahayana.

Mahayana Buddhism is the path followed in Tibet and Nepal. It is a more esoteric philosophy, blending some of the ancient Bon ideas and a phenomenon from India known as Tantra. This branch of Buddhism is known as the Vajrayana. Pure Tantra is translated as meaning 'to open the mind'. Tantra may well have developed from pagan ideas and female worship with its ritualistic cults. In Buddhism, Tantra asserts that each person is a Buddha and each can find this path within himself or herself. Tibetan Tantric Buddhism was further developed around the 11th century, giving rise to the features of the religion we see today.

Tibetan Tantric Buddhism has many themes, but most involve meditation. Some of the icons represent revered historical figures, such as Guru Rinpoche, Milarepa and Tsong Khapa, who have helped to illuminate Buddhist philosophy. Numerous other 'deities' are not gods but images that can be used to direct the mind in meditations towards a true path of learning. Fearsome protectors are not true demons, but remind the follower about his darker side and the directions to be avoided through life. Other deities can be invoked through meditation to channel the mind's energies towards the search for its true nature.

Tantric yoga is now widely known as one method of pursuing enlightenment. Recently interest has been aroused in ancient exercises, which involve sensual methods of reaching this goal. It was partly a rejection of the general liberalisation of pure Buddhism through Tantric ideas in India that led to the resurgence of Hinduism and the decline of Buddhism.

PRINCIPAL TIBETAN BUDDHIST SECTS

There are four main Buddhist sects in Tibet. Each still has a large following. (Note that the Kadam-pa have now evolved into the Gelug-pa.)

Nyingma-pa

The Nyingma-pa is the oldest Tibetan Buddhist sect; its adherents are known as the Red Hats. Its teachings are from the Vajrayana, the Tantric branch of Buddhism that came from India across the Himalayas. It developed under King Trisong Detsen, who requested the Indian master Santarakshita to teach Indian Buddhism in Tibet. In 765AD Padma Sambhava, the most famous Indian Tantric sage, was invited to Tibet by Santarakshita.

Monastery paintings

The ideas flourished and Padma Sambhava, later known as Guru Rinpoche, became the founder of Lamaism in Tibet. He is often depicted as fierce, carrying a skull-laden staff and a *vajra* (or *dorje*), the thunderbolt symbol. The deities in monasteries of the Nyingma-pa are often seen in wrathful mode, and many have their roots in the former Bonpo animistic beliefs that predate Buddhism in Tibet. The Nyingma-pa and the Bon still share many features.

Guru Rinpoche's consort Yeshe Tsogyal wrote down many of the teachings of her mentor. Most of these scriptures were concealed, but some have been revealed to Buddhist *lamas*. One scripture talks of the dark ages to come in Tibet, an era that seems now to have arrived in the Himalayan regions. Today the Nyingma-pa sect is still found in Tibet, Spiti, Ladakh, Bhutan and across the Khumbu region of Nepal around Everest.

Kadam-pa

The Kadam-pa doctrines were developed by Atisha. He was a prince, priest, teacher and intellectual from the great Buddhist university of

Narlanda in northern India. He established the sect during his studies at Toling monastery in the Guge region of western Tibet around 1040AD.

Atisha suggested that those adopting the Kadam-pa teachings should only use Tantric methods to enlightenment after careful reflection and study of the texts. The Kadam-pa doctrines refined the earlier Nyingma-pa ideas. Some believe that the austere practices of the Kadam-pa sect led to it being eclipsed later by the powerful Sakya-pa. The Kadam-pa doctrines became the basis of the Yellow Hat sect, the now-dominant Gelug-pas (see below).

Kagyu-pa

The Kagyu-pa is a sect attributed to the Indian mystic translator (Lotsawa) Marpa, a disciple of Atisha. He followed in the path of the other famous Indian sages, Tilopa and Naropa, who are also considered masters of Kagyu-pa. Marpa lived from 1012 to 1097. Marpa's student Milarepa became Kagyu-pa's great saint, as well as being a hermit and poet. Milarepa led a wild early life and practised black magic. After his awakening to Buddhist ideas, he repented his misdemeanours and went to live in isolation in the Himalayas. One of his more famous cave dwellings is near Nyalam in Tibet, just across the border from Nepal.

The Kagyu-pa adherents concentrate their meditations on inner mental and spiritual matters, and above all they follow the wisdom of their Buddhist teachers. Today the Kagyu-pa sect dominates the Kailash region. The Kagyu-pa sect split into a number of sub-groups, such as the Drigung-pa, Druk-pa, Taglung-pa and the Karma-pa. The latter, with their head monastery at Tsurphu, have become embroiled in controversy due to the dispute between the exiled Tibetan community in India and the Chinese over who is the correct reincarnate *lama* of the sect.

Sakya-pa

The Sakya-pa sect began in the 11th century. Konchok Gyalpo, who founded the Sakya monastery, was a pupil of Drogmi, who had also studied at Narlanda. This sect stresses the need for the study of existing Buddhist scriptures. Learning and study are its main themes, with a bias against the Tantric or physical elements. By 1220 the Sakya-pa was dominant in Tibet. Its main proponent was Kunga Gyetsan, a great Buddhist adherent who laid the foundations for cooperation between Tibet and Mongolia around 1247. Under the Sakya-pa, the two great Tibetan Buddhist scriptures, the Tangyur and Kangyur, were compiled. The Sakya-pa declined when Tsong Khapa, the next reformer, appeared.

Gelug-pa

The Gelug-pa is the Yellow Hat sect of the Dalai Lama. Tsong Khapa was the initiator and reformer of this sect. He

Sakyamuni Buddha

reformed the earlier ideas of Atisha in the 14th century. This form of Buddhism reverted to a more purist format. It brought a higher degree of discipline to the monastic community and put more emphasis on morality. It sought to cleanse the religion and to exorcise some of the liberal Tantric aspects. The first monastery was established at Ganden near Lhasa. The large monasteries of Drepung and Sera in Lhasa and Tashi Lhunpo in Xigatse belong to this sect. The Gelug-pa sect is now the dominant sect in Tibet and they still follow the lineage of the Dalai Lamas as spiritual leader.

Any visit to a Buddhist (or Bon) monastery is likely to be both fascinating and bewildering. Further details about the different deities and icons of both Bon and Buddhism are given in the glossary.

FESTIVALS

Visitors to Tibet may be privileged to witness a colourful festival, although these once common events are less in evidence today. In the Kailash region the festival you are most likely to see will be Saga Dawa at Tarboche on the Kailash Kora route.

All over Tibet one of the most important festivals is **Losar**, which marks the New Year. It normally falls in February (sometimes early March) on the new moon. In preparation, houses and possessions are cleaned and, as in most auspicious places or religious devotions, juniper is burnt. At monasteries and public gatherings, the monks perform rites to ward off any negative spirits connected to the old year. People rise early on the day of the New Year and are on their best behaviour, in order to make it a day of right actions, for these deeds may extend over into the coming year. Generally on the third day of the New Year people gather in a communal manner at auspicious places. In major centres Tibetan drama and masked dances can be observed.

In Lhasa, during the **Lantern** festival you may see elaborate butter sculptures in the main bazaar, the Barkhor. Celebrations associated with the **Monlam** festival have occasionally been halted by the authorities in recent years due to tensions within the community. This festival began at Ganden monastery in 1409. An image of the future Buddha, Maitreya, is carried around the Barkhor in Lhasa. At one time giant *thangka* pictures were also unfolded.

In May, or sometimes in June, the birth of the earthly Buddha, Gautama Siddhartha, the Sakyamuni Buddha, is celebrated across the country. Known as the **Saga Dawa** festival, its popularity with Tibetans may be enjoyed by trekkers to Kailash. It is also the time when the Sakyamuni Buddha experienced his enlightenment. The main feature of the festival at Kailash is the raising of the giant flagpole. The accurate placing of this pole is paramount

Buddhist festival masked dancers

Monks celebrating

to the auspicious omens for the coming year.

At a time decided by astrologers, **Guru Rinpoche's birthday** is celebrated over the August and September period. This occasion is rejoiced over particularly by followers of the Nyingma-pa, but most Tibetans join in the celebrations. Many Tibetans revere Guru Rinpoche as a second Buddha.

In September or October, the **Wanghor** festival, which probably originated as a Bon tradition, celebrates the coming of the harvest. It has always been linked to the offering of devotions to the earth for a good crop. The earth spirits need to be honoured for good luck.

During November and December, Tibetans celebrate the **Lhabab Duchen** festival, which commemorates the Buddha's descent from heaven. Also at this time they commemorate the great patron of the Gelug-pa, **Tsong Khapa**, with a festival involving various processions.

Cham dances are performed at different times of the year and involved many masked dances. The Black Hat dance is one of the more important on these occasions. Some of the dances are enacted to celebrate the victory of Buddhism over Bon. Various forms of dance have been performed since the time of Guru Rinpoche; most are derived from the earliest Tantric rituals. These Tantric associations are supposed to stimulate the inner mind, to turn it away from unhealthy forces like anger and create a soul full of compassionate forces.

OFFICIAL HOLIDAYS			
1 January	New Year	1 July	Founding of the Communist Party
February/March	Tibetan New Year (Losar)	1 August	Founding of the People's Liberation Army
1 May	Labour Day	1 October	National Day
4 May	Youth Day		

Some of the dances and side charades are extremely funny to watch, with mocking of the crowd, and amusing characters like Mi Tsering, the goblin-like clown seen in Nepal.

A FEW CULTURAL CONSIDERATIONS

When visiting monasteries, trekking hats and boots should be removed before entry. In such a climate, an inappropriate state of partial undress is unlikely to be an issue! Small donations are appreciated in monasteries and photographers should ask before taking pictures inside. On the trail, keep to the left of *mani* walls and *chortens* and circle them in a clockwise direction.

Toilet paper should be burnt along the trails and rubbish carried out. Begging is not a common activity in Tibet, but tipping, although not part of the local tradition, is appreciated by porters, guides and staff on organised trips.

Buddhist monks at Boudhanath, Kathmandu

PRE-DEPARTURE PREPARATION

TREKKING SEASONS

A trek to Kailash is best undertaken in either spring or autumn, although pilgrims visit the mountain in a steady stream between May and September. Trekking at the height of summer, July and August, is likely to be frustrating for those hoping to see the mountain vistas and Kailash's peak. Cloud, rain and snow can be expected at any time from mid-June to mid-September. With hundreds of Hindu pilgrims on the circuit, conditions will not offer a great deal of solitude to recreational walkers.

That leaves two windows for those set on seeing as much of the mountain scenery as possible. The spring season – late April, May and early June – is the most popular trekking season at present. The weather is generally stable, although clouds are likely to cover some of the mountains at times. Wind tends to be a factor at this time of year and can considerably lower ambient temperatures. That said, wind can occur at any time of year, so adequate clothing is vitally important. The Saga Dawa festival in May or June is the busiest period for western visitors, but the bonus of a rare Tibetan cultural experience more than compensates for the additional numbers.

The autumn season from mid-September until late October is another good time to visit the region. In

Himalayas from the north (from the Lalung La pass)

fact this season probably offers the best clarity for observing the stunning Tibetan landscapes. October sees far fewer Hindu pilgrims, but hardy Tibetans may well be encountered. Trekkers in late October may well be alone, but expect the temporary nomad refreshment tents to be leaving by about 28 October, or earlier if the weather has deteriorated. October can be simply stunning when the weather is stable, with crystal-clear skies. Photographers might well gamble on visiting then. As a rule the wind can be less of a problem at this time.

However, in some years October weather can be fickle, and this is the main drawback. Snowstorms can temporarily close the passes on the road to Kailash at any time in October. This can of course wreak havoc with strictly limited itineraries, so you would be wise to add in extra days at this time when possible. For those willing to accept the risk of these erratic storms, October is probably worth the risk. Lucky visitors will experience a special place at its glittering best.

Snow may be found on the highest point of the circuit, the Drolma La pass (5660m), at any time of the trekking season. Strong winds here will be a major distraction, and the effects of the windchill factor at this point cannot be overstated.

Those hoping to visit Toling and Tsaparang should take note of the above conditions. In general, access routes to Toling remain open due to the presence of military installations in the border regions. Summer is not a good time to visit, so plan on a spring or autumn trip. In early spring, roads may be disrupted by snow meltwaters in places, but this may not be a great inconvenience. The autumn period, which is usually stable, is probably the optimum period so long as there are no unseasonal storms.

See 'Climate' for more detail.

STYLE OF TREK

The type of trek or tour you may be considering will dictate the itinerary. There are three options and these are discussed below.

Fully supported group treks

For most this is the preferred option, and these trips provide the maximum security for visitors. The tour operator removes many of the difficulties and discomforts associated with other ways of organising this trek. Visas and permits can be easily procured, transport does not have to be considered and all the day-to-day logistics, such as accommodation, food and carriage of baggage, are taken care of. Most trips will be fully inclusive, with few extras to add to the cost. Clients can relax and admire the scenery en route knowing that they can hike around Kailash in as much comfort as is possible in such a remote place.

That said, there are some disadvantages. Large groups with the support of a Nepali crew often take a

Tingri plains, group campsite

truck to carry the equipment, food, extra staff and so on and these Chinese-built, ageing machines can sometimes be much slower than the 4x4 vehicles used for the clients. It might be that clients have to wait at camp for the cooks and gear to arrive much later. A major disadvantage is that there is less flexibility on a pre-organised itinerary (although most visits are highly regimented by the Chinese anyway). You may also be hiking with fellow travellers who have underestimated the challenges and may not be in the best of spirits. In general, though, most hikers enjoy the conviviality of like-minded fellow walkers.

One other unnecessary danger is the possible effect of 'peer pressure' within the group. At its worst this can overrule common sense, with some members ignoring their symptoms of altitude sickness in the unacknowledged race to compete. Do not fall into this lethal trap.

See Appendix 6 for tour operators offering fully inclusive group trips.

Independently organised trips with a local trek operator

For those with more time, and who do not want to be locked into the group ethos, this might be a good option. Participants will be able to set out their preferred itinerary, what they wish to include, the length of trip and any other special interest options. Organising a trip through an agent in the UK, Nepal or even Tibet for a couple or a small group may well be more expensive than a group departure, but not necessarily so. Comfort could be compromised to avoid higher costs. The number in the group is critical, because each car can only comfortably take three with a driver and guide. A fourth person might drastically add to the cost, unless the driver acts as guide for example.

This type of trip offers a great deal of freedom, but there is an increased risk if only one car is used. Heading to Toling probably increases the risk, as the roads are little used. We met only one or two other vehicles during our two days' driving there. That said, the military are always around and a good agent will carry mobile phones that work near settlements. As hinted at above, it is possible to cut costs. By not taking a Nepali cooking crew and staying in rough-and-ready guesthouses, a few hundred dollars can be saved. Taking this option will mean bringing substantial amounts of food from home in order to minimise the problem of poor and limited local food choices.

Contacting a local operator in Lhasa directly should be straightforward, although they seem to take a while to reply. If you choose to arrange the trip directly with a Lhasa agent, you might well want to fly into Lhasa to finalise the trip and pay the operators. Those planning on entering from Nepal would be better advised to contact a Nepalese agent to sort out the trip with their colleagues in Lhasa, because it will still be necessary to enlist the services of a Nepalese agent to arrange the visa from the Chinese embassy in Kathmandu. A pre-arranged 'group' visa issued here can be for as few as two people.

See Appendix 6 for a list of local agents.

Completely independent travel

This is quite a rare choice these days in Tibet. The Chinese are not keen on such adventurous travel and, considering the nature of the terrain, one can appreciate why this should be so. However, those who have a lot of experience of travel in the developing world, or even those with a lot of spirit, might look into this option. The main snag with this sort of trip is that you cannot rely on obtaining a visa in Kathmandu because they issue only group visas. It is possible to arrange a

Paryang locals outside the lodge (Saga to Paryang)

package tour to Lhasa in Kathmandu and then attempt to extend the visa in Lhasa, but this is not a guaranteed option at present. A better option is to get a visa in your home country, or even better in Hong Kong, and then enter Tibet from the mainland area via Golmud or Chengdu by plane. (See 'Visas and permits'.)

Once in Lhasa it should be possible to hire a car with some fellow travellers. This is usually the cheapest option for renting cars and drivers. Some very hardy travellers have brought in mountain bicycles and pedalled all over Tibet. A few lucky travellers have hitchhiked with local truck drivers, but this can mean problems for the truck drivers and they are more reluctant to do this now.

The rates for hiring a 4x4 vehicle are approximately 3.5–4 Yuan per kilometre. (See 'Money matters' for exchange rates at the time of writing.) You need to add a further 50 per cent to cover the cost of the return of the car to Lhasa if the journey is one way (for example, from Lhasa to Kailash and then to the Nepalese border). Guides will cost around 150 Yuan per day.

See Appendix 6 for a list of agencies in Lhasa.

ACCOMMODATION AND FOOD

The style and condition of accommodation used in western Tibet will naturally depend on the sort of trip chosen. The majority of groups will be **camping** around Kailash. En route to the mountain, many parties camp, but

Village children (Saga to Paryang)

some may stay at guesthouses or in the limited hotels. Travelling from Kathmandu, the only reasonable hotels are in Zhangmu, Nyalam, Saga and Toling, though even these suffer from the vagaries of poor plumbing. Hot water might be available if you're lucky, but not heating.

Good to excellent **hotels** are now available in Lhasa. Xigatse and Gyangtse now have at least one good hotel each. Elsewhere, the Tibetan-style **guesthouses**, while atmospheric, have basic rooms, often with four or more beds. Beds are hard and bedding of dubious cleanliness. Rooms, while nicely decorated, are small, almost cosy but very cold. The family kitchen, the warmest room, is often used for eating; visitors can luxuriate on carpeted seats and take in the flavour of life on the plateau in all its facets.

Washing

All hotels will provide a thermos of hot water, although you may have to ask for it. They also usually provide china cups, and sometimes even saucers, for your afternoon tea! You will also normally be provided with a large bowl. Have your tea first, in the smart china cups, then you can use the rest of the water for washing. Don't even think about asking for a hot shower, except perhaps in Saga or Zhangmu!

Toilets

These will provide endless conversation throughout any trip. Most are outside, often up small steep steps and open to the stars – their only advantage. Up to three holes in the floor might be provided. Assuming you don't need three holes, expect other guests to squat beside you. And

Bob's self-service meal at Paryang (Paryang to Saga)

be very careful not to drop any valuables down the holes! Those with a delicate disposition should consider camping, where toilet tents are provided, or take a trip to the Maldives instead.

Food

A liking for noodles would be a great advantage. Lhasa now has a good variety of food options, but elsewhere don't anticipate too many treats. In the small towns, Xigatse, Gyangtse, Nyalam and Saga, you will find acceptable Chinese fare. Toling too has a couple of good places. Most visitors on inclusive trips will be catered for, with probably adequate supplies if your crew is Nepalese. If not, take your own supplies. Muesli is a good filler, even with boiled water. Also consider taking dried potato, instant soups and tinned fish or meat. Everyone should take chocolate, energy bars and snacks to relieve the monotony of noodles. See 'Equipment' for lists of what to take.

The further you get from civilisation, the less choice there is, but by this time anything begins to taste good!

Kathmandu is a returning trekker's paradise, a Shangri-la of indulgence. A reasonable meal will cost from 200–500 Nepalese rupees per person for a main dish, pizza, steak, or curry. (See 'Money matters' for exchange rates.) In Tibet meals are slightly more expensive.

VISAS AND PERMITS

Chinese visas

In order to visit Tibet and China, it is currently necessary to obtain a Chinese visa. Applying in your own country is easier if you intend to travel to Tibet from the Chinese heartlands. Visas issued in Europe are normally valid for one month. It may now be necessary to show proof of onward travel (with an air ticket).

As a rule, visas obtained in Hong Kong are issued for longer periods on request. This is the best solution for those planning extended stays in Tibet and hoping to move about freely. It normally takes up to three days to get a 60–90 day visa and costs about 380 Hong Kong dollars. For an extra fee you can get it faster, even the same day.

Special arrangements are required for those arriving in Tibet from Nepal. Visas are normally issued only for the duration of the stated itinerary, with extensions not always possible. The visa may well be issued on a piece of paper and not stamped into the passport. In theory, a group visa is issued to no less than four members, but they can be obtained for groups as small as two. It is wise to allow at least a couple of days in Kathmandu before your departure for the Chinese border and the application process should be done well in advance, before arrival in Nepal for those with limited time. If you are arranging the visa in Nepal in conjunction with a Nepalese agent, you will be required to submit details through the local agent to Lhasa for

Xixapangma north face, sunset (Xixapangma Trekking Routes)

approval before the visa process is begun. This could require a week or so in Kathmandu, unless arranged before arrival by email through the Nepalese agent.

As for other permits, this matter gets rather grey and is subject to frequent changes. Those on group visas and those with visas issued in Kathmandu will be given all the necessary road permits and town permits through the embassy at the same time as the visa arrangements. Be sure to list all the towns and destinations you hope to visit when applying. This is very important for those wishing to visit the Zanda/Toling–Tsaparang region.

Those arriving in Lhasa from Chengdu, Golmud and other cities in China will have to visit the Public Security Bureau (PSB) in Lhasa to request any permits required. As this is subject to change, often at short notice, a visit to the PSB is recommended before attempting any further travel or arrangements.

Chinese embassies

UK 31 Portland Place, London W1B 1QD; tel: 020 7631 1430 (2.00pm–4.00pm, Monday to Friday); fax: 020 7436 9178; www.chinese-embassy.org.uk

USA 2201 Wisconsin Ave NW, Suite 110, Washington DC 20007; tel: 202 338 6688; fax: 202 588 9760; www.china-embassy.org/eng

Australia 15 Coronation Drive, Yarralumla, Canberra, 2600 ACT; tel: 2 6273 4783/2 6273 7443

(9.00am–12.30pm, Monday to Friday); fax: 02 6273 9615; http://au.china-embassy.org/eng/

India 50-D Shantipath, Chanakyapuri, New Delhi, 110121 India; tel: 011 2467 5559; fax: 011 2611 1105; www.chinaembassy.org.in

Nepal Baluwatar, Kathmandu; tel: 1 4419053 (9.30am – 11.00am only); fax: 1 4414045; www.chinaembassy.org.np

Hong Kong Visa Office, Low Block 5th Floor China Building, 26 Harbour Road, Wanchai, Hong Kong; tel: 2585 1794 or 2585 1700

Note that telephone numbers above are without international country codes. If phoning from abroad you should add the international access code (00 if calling from the UK) and then the country code and finally the number quoted, omitting any initial zero. County dialling codes are as follows: UK 44; USA 1; Australia 61; India 91; Nepal 977; China 86; Hong Kong 852.

See Appendix 6 for other Chinese embassies.

Nepalese visas

All foreign nationals except Indians require an entry visa. Currently visas are available from embassies and at Tribhuvan International Airport on arrival in Kathmandu (check for any changes before arrival). Land borders are at Sonauli/Belahiya, near Bhairahawa, if travelling from Gorakhpur, at Raxaul/Birgunj, Nepalganj, Mahendranagar (West Nepal/Tanakpur) and Kakarvitta (Darjeeling/Siliguri to West Bengal). Accessing the remoter crossing points may be subject to change with the unpredictable political difficulties in some of these districts.

Visa fees change constantly, but are currently as follows:

- First entry in a calendar year, two months: US$30.
- Subsequent entries within the same calendar year, one month: US$30.
- Multiple entry: US$50 extra.
- Transit visas, up to three days: free.

Also, if your first visit to Nepal was for more than 15 days, on your second visit you will be given a free visa, though it is unclear how long this might last. So if you have the time, spend a couple of weeks in Kathmandu before you go to Tibet, and you can get back into paradise free of charge!

Nepalese embassies

UK 12A Kensington Palace Gardens, London W8 4QU; tel: 020 7229 1594/020 7229 6231/020 7229 5352; fax: 020 7792 9861; info@nepembassy.org.uk; www.nepembassy.org.uk

NOTE ON THE POLITICAL SITUATION IN NEPAL

The dispute between the Royal Palace, the politicians and the Maoist rebels has created an uncertain situation in Nepal. After King Gyanendra relinquished absolute power in April 2006, the country became more settled, though there followed a lot of political wrangling between the different parties, known as the SPP (Seven Political Parties) and the Maoists.

Under United Nations auspices, the Maoists and the Nepal Army (no longer 'Royal') handed in their weapons. An Interim Government including the Maoists is now in power, and the future of the monarchy is in doubt.

As we write, free elections are planned for 2007. Should you be in the country in the run-up to the elections, be aware that demonstrations and strikes may be called at short notice. In case they suddenly turn violent, you are advised to avoid all large gatherings and remain vigilant at all times.

It is to be hoped that the country will soon return to a peaceful situation, and that tourists will again be permitted to visit the more remote regions, like Simikot in the west, where development is sorely needed. In any event, even during the worst of the troubles, no foreign tourist was harmed in Nepal. For the latest Foreign Office travel advice on Nepal, visit www.fco.gov.uk/travel.

USA 2131 Leroy Place, NW, Washington, DC 20008; tel: 202 667 4550; fax: 202 667 5534; info@nepalembassyusa.org; www.nepalembassyusa.org

India Barakhamba Road, New Delhi, 110001, India; tel: 011 332 9969; fax: 011 3326857; ramjanki@del2.vsnl.net.in

China 1 Sanlitunlu Xilujie, Beijing, People's Republic of China; tel: 01 532 1795; fax: 01 532 3251

Tibet (consulate) Nepalese Consulate General, Norbulingka Road 13, Lhasa, Tibet Autonomous Region of the People's Republic of China; tel: 0891 682 2881/683 6890; fax: 0891 683 6890

Hong Kong (consulate) Nepalese Consulate General, Unit 1206, Greenfield Tower, Concordia Plaza, 1 Science Museum Road, Tsim Sha Tsui, East Kowloon, Hong Kong; tel: 2369 7813; fax: 2824 2970; rncghk@datainternet.com

MONEY MATTERS

The currency in China and Tibet is the Renminbi (or Yuan). The main notes are in the following denominations: 5, 10, 20, 50, 100. Fen are the smaller denomination used in this region.

The currency in Nepal is the Nepalese Rupee. Notes used are in the following denominations: 5, 10, 20, 50, 100, 500 and 1000. There are coins for 1, 2 and 5 rupees.

Banks and ATMs

Changing money, cash and travellers cheques is reasonably easy in **Lhasa** and **Xigatse**. Those travelling directly to Kailash from Nepal can change money with street dealers in **Zhangmu** close to the immigration department. They exchange cash US dollars and Nepalese rupees as a rule. The Bank of China at the top of Zhangmu also changes money at slightly better rates, but it takes longer. Cash and travellers cheques can be changed here. Bear in mind that there is little to spend money on if you are on an inclusive trip. The main expense is staff tipping, an occasional souvenir and possibly entry fees to Tsaparang/Toling. Few visitors will be 'eating out'.

APPROXIMATE EXCHANGE RATES (IN APRIL 2007)

	Chinese Yuan	Nepalese Rupee
£	14.0	135
€	9.6	89
US$	8.0	70
CHF (Swiss francs)	10.0	60

ATMs are now quite common in **Kathmandu**. In Thamel there is one in the Kathmandu Guest House courtyard and next door close to Greenhill Travels. Another option is a cash advance at the Himalayan Bank on Tri Devi Marg.

Money changers are very quick for cash or travellers cheques and rates are very little lower than banks. Banks also change money, but are generally slow.

HEALTH MATTERS

The main problems when discussing health matters in Tibet are the remoteness of the Kailash region, and the high altitude. It cannot be emphasised enough that there are **virtually no adequate medical facilities** en route. The nearest serviceable hospital is in Ali to the northwest, some 300 miles away. A very basic clinic is said to exist in Toling (Zanda), and of course the military have some facilities, which may or may not be available to visitors in extreme cases. Evacuation has been done in the past via western Nepal. Sick guests are ferried by road to the Nepal border via Purang and then a military or private helicopter is dispatched at vast expense from Kathmandu. In the past the border region and Simikot have sometimes been closed to foreigners, because of the conflict with Maoist insurgents. Now there is peace, it is hoped that access to the region will be permitted throughout the Kailash season.

Although of some concern, any prospective visitor should not be unduly worried about the health risks if only visiting Lhasa and its immediate environs.

With relatively fewer bugs living at high altitude, Tibet is not as unhealthy as some more popular destinations, provided you are careful with personal hygiene and what you eat. That said, local standards of hygiene are appalling by western standards.

The following practices have been found to reduce health problems significantly:

- never drink untreated tap water
- avoid salads
- peel fruits
- brush teeth in bottled water, and wash hands regularly.

Water sterilisation

The biggest problems are concerned with the lack of running water. Keeping hands clean is paramount in order to avoid the more common ailments. Fortunately all guesthouses in Tibet, however primitive, will provide boiled water thermos flasks for guests. Those on group treks in Nepal, coming from Simikot, will have access to plentiful boiled water. Very useful in the absence of washing facilities are *wet wipes* for hands and largish *baby wipes* for other parts! Bring plastic bags to keep used items and pack out all such rubbish.

With a supply of boiled water in thermos flasks in Tibet, the difficulty of obtaining safe drinking water is alleviated considerably, so long as the water comes freshly boiled. Water boils at a lower temperature on the plateau, so some may wish to add water sterilising tablets to the water as an added precaution. Iodine tablets or Micropur can be used. Bottled drinking water can also be bought in Nyalam, Saga, Toling and Darchen in season, but bring an initial supply from Kathmandu or Lhasa.

Vaccination suggestions

Visitors to Tibet or Nepal should note

VACCINATIONS

Cholera vaccination, although not very effective or required by law, might be recommended if any recent outbreak has occurred.

Typhoid and **paratyphoid** vaccinations are strongly recommended, as these diseases are potential risks.

Yellow fever vaccination will give cover for ten years. It is normally only required if coming from an infected area.

Tetanus and **polio** vaccinations are also recommended.

BCG tuberculosis injections may also be recommended by some GPs.

Hepatitis A is the main Hepatitis risk for travellers and a long term vaccination for this is available.

that no vaccinations are currently legally required. However this should always be checked with your doctor before travel in case of any changes. Other advice is available through the Medical Advisory Service for Travellers Abroad (MASTA) at www.masta-travel-health.com.

Sporadic outbreaks of **meningitis** and **Japanese encephalitis** occur in rural parts of Tibet and Nepal, although the risk is minimal. Vaccines are available, but are expensive. The Himalayan Clinic in Kathmandu gives vaccinations for these at short notice for a negotiable fee! The CIWEC clinic is another good option in Kathmandu.

Rabies is certainly found in Tibet and Nepal, but unless you expect to make prolonged or frequent visits to these countries, vaccination is an expensive procedure to embark on. However, anyone concerned about rabies should seek advice at least six months at least before the planned trip. Beware of dogs in Tibet, particularly those that guard nomad settlements and even monasteries. Being aware of this menace is half way to prevention.

Malaria prophylaxis

Malaria is not found in central, northern or western Tibet. In Nepal, malaria is at present confined to the southern lowlands. Those however spending a night in Nepalganj en route to Simikot will be exposed to malarial risks. This is a real inconvenience and the risks should not be ignored. For anyone visiting the Chitwan National Park in southern Nepal as a side trip after Tibet, the risk should be considered.

Currently the use of the daily tablet Paludrine in combination with a weekly course of chloroquine (Avloclor or Nivaquine) is recommended. Both tablets must be started a week before entering a risk zone and taken for four to six weeks after leaving. Another drug used is Malarone. Doxycycline can be taken as a prophylactic by anyone allergic to other drugs. Lariam is another possibility, but it can have very nasty side effects on some people, and it would be wise to test it out before travel, so get a couple of tablets first to check. Consult your GP about a suitable course, since recommendations change constantly. The use of insect repellent at and after dusk will help prevent bites.

It is vital to consult your GP about which vaccinations you require, and allow plenty of time for the whole series of vaccinations, as they cannot all be given at the same time. It is worthwhile ensuring that all your vaccinations are recorded on a certificate, although this is not a legal requirement.

Other nasty bugs

Giardia Lamblia is another bug to watch out for, but there is no preventative treatment apart from careful eating and drinking. It is contracted mostly through drinking infected water. It strikes the digestive tract and lives in its host until arrested by a course of Flagyl (Metronidazole) or Tinidazole. This nasty bug manifests itself as sulphurous foul-smelling gases, cramp and sometimes diarrhoea.

Dengue Fever is occasionally reported in Nepal, but the risk is very low in Kathmandu. There is no treatment other than rest and avoidance of mosquitoes.

Common ailments

The most common ailments are colds, blocked sinuses, headaches and stomach disorders.

In the event of stomach upsets, the use of Imodium or Lomotil is recommended initially if symptoms are not serious, and also during the long road journeys for convenience. The antibiotic drugs norfloxacin and ciprofloxacin may be used in more debilitating cases. These are available in Kathmandu. It is necessary to drink more liquids in dry regions. Dioralyte will help rehydration in cases of fluid loss due to stomach upsets. This can be found in Nepal in packets called Jeevan Jal.

A good supply of painkillers for headaches should always be carried in Tibet, where the altitude causes them most frequently at the beginning of a trip. Remedies for blocked noses, sore throats, coughs and sneezes should be easily accessible in any medical kit. The dry air often causes irritations. Available over the counter at chemists are Sudafed, Mucron, Strepsils and similar products.

Stemetil can be used for those prone to carsickness.

Finally, don't under estimate the power of the sun at high altitude, despite cold temperatures. You should always take sunscreen with you.

Dental care

You should visit your dentist for a check-up before the trip, unless you want to rely on the 'tooth temple god' in Kathmandu for treatment. There are now also some highly competent dentists in Kathmandu, but you are unlikely to meet one in Tibet.

Clinics

You should also check with your GP and with one of the specialised clinics listed overleaf for the latest updated medical advice for travellers.

First aid kit

The following list is not exhaustive but an indication of requirements:

- Aspirin/paracetamol
- Antiseptic cream
- Dressings
- Scissors
- Eyewash
- Stomach upset remedies
- Dioralyte rehydration sachets
- Insect repellent
- Antihistamine cream
- Water sterilising tablets (Micropur or iodine)
- Safety pins
- Wet wipes
- Antibiotic general course
- Personal medications

International Society of Travel Medicine www.istm.org

Hospital for Tropical Diseases Travel Clinic Mortimer Market Building, Capper Street, London WC1E 6AU; tel: 020 7388 9600; www.thehtd.org. Also runs a premium line service 0906 133 7733 for individual country queries.

MASTA (Medical Advisory Service for Travellers Abroad), London School of Hygiene and Tropical Medicine, Keppel Street, London WC1 7HT; tel: 0906 550 1402; enquiries@masta.org. MASTA currently have several clinics around the UK, and you can call 0870 241 6843 to find the nearest, or look online at www.masta-travel-health.com.

NHS Travel website www.fitfortravel.scot.nhs.uk for advice on immunisations and malaria.

Himalayan Clinic Jyatha, Thamel, Kathmandu offers sterile packed vaccinations.

CIWEC Clinic Kathmandu is an excellent medical centre.

For altitude sickness

- Diamox
- Coca tablets
- Ginkgo Biloba

After reading this you may become a hypochondriac before you even get to Tibet, but if you do not prepare for almost every eventuality, your only alternative may be the somewhat unconventional Tibetan medical cures.

MOUNTAIN SICKNESS/ALTITUDE

What is altitude sickness?

Altitude sickness is a condition that can affect anyone, young or old, who spends time above 3000m. In a few rare cases those intolerant to altitude can experience symptoms at a lower level, as low as 2600m. However, for most trekkers a level of around 3400m is when symptoms begin to arise. One of the main factors causing the condition is the lowering of the oxygen content within the atmosphere, which is more drastic with ever higher levels. The body needs to increase the flow of oxygen to the brain via the bloodstream and lungs. To do this, more red blood cells are produced, though this process may take a week or more. The pulse rate also increases, as does the rate of breathing. Starved of oxygen, the human body begins to suffer in several ways.

There are three categories of altitude sickness:

- **AMS** Acute Mountain Sickness, which is very common, but not necessarily life-threatening if it is treated correctly. The point at which someone is suffering this level of sickness is hard to evaluate. As a rule it can be diagnosed once symptoms fail to disappear at a constant elevation. Going higher could induce one or both of the following:
- **HAPE** High Altitude Pulmonary Oedema is when fluid collects in the lungs. It is characterised by gurgling sounds in the chest. This condition can be fatal if ignored.
- **HACE** High Altitude Cerebral Oedema is when fluid collects in the brain. This condition can be fatal and can develop quickly if ignored.

We recommend that you learn as much as you can about the effects of altitude before you go, and check out the medicines on offer to aid acclimatisation (see 'Options from the pharmacist' below). See also *Pocket First Aid and Wilderness Medicine* (Cicerone).

The main early symptoms of altitude are **headaches**, **nausea**, **tiredness**, **lack of appetite** and later **disorientation**. These in themselves are not a reason to stop the trek, but are good indicators of problems that may be overcome by taking a rest when necessary. Difficulty is often experienced with sleeping. Breathing patterns may be erratic (Cheyne-Stokes breathing) and the heart might thump a bit disconcertingly; however, these are not unusual effects. One important thing to remember is that the symptoms of attitude do not manifest immediately on reaching a camp or lodge, but tend to appear an hour or more after arrival. For this reason you should not start walking about exploring the new location, but should sit calmly for a while, take tea, fluids and rest. Those flying into Lhasa should refrain from rushing off to see the attractions for a few hours.

Continuing to ascend with any persistent symptoms can lead to the serious risk of **Pulmonary (HAPE)** and **Cerebral Oedema (HACE)** or even **death**. There are deaths each year in Tibet and Nepal from altitude sickness, despite all the warnings. Sometimes complications from altitude sickness can strike very quickly. Yamantaka is the deity of death; don't seek him out!

In order to minimise the effects of altitude, proceed to higher elevations in incremental steps of no more than 300m per day for optimum comfort and safety. Where this is not practical, err on the side of caution when planning an itinerary in Tibet. It is impossible to predict how anyone will adjust to altitude in advance; even if you have been to higher altitude before, you might suffer altitude sickness at a lower altitude on another occasion.

In our personal experience over many years in the Himalayas, we have noticed that many trekkers have mild symptoms of altitude sickness at about 3400m. A day's rest at this level is normally enough for most to find the symptoms disappear and they can continue upwards. Another critical level appears to be around 4500m, where another day of rest, or at least sleep, at the same altitude is necessary. Above this level it is harder to predict the effects, but by going no more than 300m up each subsequent day most people can manage to keep symptoms at bay.

Don't forget that it is dangerous to overexert on arrival at any destination, thinking you have no symptoms, as their appearance is often delayed.

Altitude problems specific to Tibet

Normally in the Himalayas the rule is 'Descending is the only safe cure, at any time of day or night.'

However, Tibet is an exception, primarily because descent is not physically possible in most places. In order to minimise the risk of suffering from altitude sickness, it is therefore of the utmost importance to acclimatise before going higher. For this reason, many group treks to Kailash spend a while acclimatising on a trek in Nepal before ascending to the Tibetan plateau. This trek should aim to be at least in the zones around 4000m altitude, and preferably above. A week-long trek in the Langtang region north of Kathmandu is one option in Nepal; the Rolwaling area is another.

Within Tibet, and perhaps a good choice for an extra day or two, is the valley south of Xixapangma. Visitors unable to do this must plan at least one extra night in Nyalam, or better still another rest day in Saga before proceeding into the remoter, high region west of Saga.

From the point of view of improving altitude acclimatisation even further for the Kailash Kora, the three-day option described later in this book, visiting Tsaparang and Toling in the ancient Guge kingdom, is best done **before** the main Kora trek. The region lies at an approximate altitude of 3800m. The dramatic scenery and cultural interest make it a great acclimatisation option.

If you do need to descend, or in the worst case evacuate, the only other route in which a descent is possible from the Kailash region is crossing into western Nepal and following the reverse of the route from Simikot, described in this book. Helicopter rescue once across the border in Nepal is an option that has been possible recently and may be a reassuring last resort.

Of all the regions in Tibet, it is in the higher western regions that more serious altitude problems can occur. Those flying into Lhasa can expect mild discomfort initially, but generally no more than a headache or lethargy. Oxygen is available in the better hotels in Lhasa. Coming from western Nepal to Kailash, a trekker may still notice some symptoms, because the walking route from Simikot is generally below 4000m and Darchen, the starting point for Kailash, is around 4650m. Those at most risk are visitors driving directly from Kathmandu (1317m) to Nyalam (3750m) and continuing on to Saga (4280m).

Once on a trek it is particularly important to walk very slowly, especially when climbing any hill. At all times avoid any hurried walking. Be sure to admit any problems (if only to yourself at first), and don't be pressurised by your trekking peers. **Altitude sickness can kill**. If you experience any serious effects before the pass on the Kailash Kora trek, you should consider returning to Darchen, where there is a basic clinic. Carrying on with mild symptoms, perhaps just a mild headache, is acceptable so long as it does not get worse or persist all day and night. The night at Driraphuk before the pass will determine how well you are acclimatised, although few will sleep well here. Virtually all westerners will feel the effects of altitude climbing the Drolma La pass; some may well feel nauseous and extremely lethargic. This is fairly normal, but symptoms will improve on the descent, so don't worry unduly.

The best way to minimise the effects of altitude in Tibet is to plan sufficient rest days into the itinerary before getting above 4500m. See Appendix 3 for suggested itineraries.

Options from the pharmacist

So what else can you do to ward off the effects of altitude? There are a few options. Many trekkers start a course of **Diamox** (Acetazolamide), a diuretic which thins the blood, makes you urinate more and is generally considered to be of some benefit, though it can have the disturbing side effect of pins and needles in the fingers. Another option is to try **Coca**. Not the smoking variety, but a version of the substance used by natives of Peru and Bolivia. Coca is available as homeopathic tablets that some trekkers swear by. It can be difficult to locate these tablets in the UK but French pharmacies stock them, should you be limbering up in the Alps before your trip. Also recommended by some are **Ginkgo Biloba** tablets, which do appear to work. It is suggested that these can be taken twice a day for five days before arrival and one tablet a day during the trek, but consult your GP before embarking on a course of these tablets as they can have serious side effects and are not suitable for everyone.

Paracetamol is good for the initial relatively mild headaches which many people will experience. For more severe HAPE or HACE altitude sickness, the only real solution is to get the patient to a lower altitude as fast as possible. In the meantime, with qualified medical assistance, **Nifedipine** or **Dexamethasone** may be used, but these are serious drugs and should not be used lightly.

Hyperbaric bag and oxygen cylinders

A hyperbaric bag (Gamow is one common brand) is a large plastic bag into which a person suffering from serious altitude sickness can be cocooned under higher air pressure to mimic a lower altitude for a limited period. Mountaineers have of course used oxygen cylinders at altitude for years. If you are with a trekking group, your staff should have these vital pieces of equipment and know how to use them. Don't be afraid to ask the crew before you leave; it could save your life. If you are travelling independently, you should seriously consider hiring such equipment in Kathmandu – and make sure it works!

MOUNTAIN SAFETY

All mountain walking presents hazards, but with prior awareness and concentration during your trek they can be minimised.

In Tibet the biggest danger in the mountains comes from the high altitude, severe cold and bitter winds. Be sure to keep well wrapped up first thing in the morning and make sure you are carrying enough warm clothing for the whole day. Remember most trekkers will not be carrying all their baggage and it will not be accessible during the walk. In the deep canyons the sun sets very early in the afternoon and temperatures plummet.

Take particular care on the rough and rocky trails; bear in mind that the nearest hospital is hundreds of miles away. Remember that you may not be thinking as clearly as normal at these

Drongba village (Saga to Paryang)

altitudes; don't take unnecessary chances, such as leaping carelessly across rivers or boulders.

Dehydration is another factor easily overlooked; you may not necessarily feel thirsty in these conditions. Taking note of the colour of your urine is one good way to keep these problems in check. If it is too yellow, you are not drinking enough. Breathing through a scarf at higher altitudes helps to retain some of the fluid that would otherwise be lost as moisture in the exhaled breath. It also keeps away some of the dust and icy winds.

Other dangers in Tibet (and Nepal) are dogs. Nomads in Tibet train their dogs to be guardians. During the day these dogs are generally docile and easily controlled by their proud owners. In guesthouses, beware of a night-time visit to the toilet. Better still, plan not to go out at all at night, and improvise some sort of suitable receptacle. Choose a large-necked plastic container, and make sure the lid seal is good!

Finally, make sure that your medical and travel insurance is adequate to cover the rough and remote conditions that you will encounter in this part of the Himalayas. This should include evacuation by air ambulance.

But don't be put off; just take care and enjoy the trek! Forewarned is forearmed.

EQUIPMENT AND SUPPLIES

The following list is a guideline only:

Clothing

- Trousers
- Jeans
- T-shirts
- Blouses
- Cotton skirts
- Socks
- Trainers
- Boots
- Underwear (thermal)
- Soft shoes
- Fleece
- Waterproof jacket
- Warm sweater
- Scarf
- Sun hat
- Woollen hat
- Duvet jacket (as thick as possible)
- Down trousers

Other supplies

- Camera
- Film
- Plastic bags
- Toilet rolls
- Torch (flashlight)
- Sunglasses
- Washing kit
- Bath plug
- Toothbrush
- Toothpaste
- Sun cream
- Lip cream
- Water bottle
- Ear plugs
- Sleeping bag (suitable down to at least -10°C)
- Sheet liner
- Penknife
- Tin opener
- Batteries for camera and torch

FOOD

You are strongly advised to take the following and any extra goodies that you particularly enjoy. They will taste extra special in Tibet!

- chocolate bars
- muesli bars
- power bars for energy
- glucose tablets

Those not taking a Nepalese cooking crew will want to take the following to supplement the meagre Tibetan and Chinese diet. These items can be 'cooked' in boiled water from thermoses or eaten raw:

- instant soups
- instant potato
- muesli (eaten with water or powdered fruit juice)
- tinned fish or meat.

MAPS

For those entering Tibet from Nepal, a varied selection of maps is available. Although they give a good picture of the routes and features, none of these maps is very accurate. In particular, there is considerable confusion over the name of the eastern peak guarding the Kangyam Glacier. Across a majority of books as well as other maps, the consensus is that it is Jampelyang (Manjushri).

In Kathmandu, try Pilgrims Book House (next to the Kathmandu Guest House), which has a vast array of maps and books on all aspects of Tibet.

Maps available are:

- **Kailash Trekkingkarte** 1:50,000. Karto Atelier, a Swiss/Nepali produced map; email: karto-atelier@bluewin.ch or karto@wlink.com.np; www.karto-atelier.com
- **Kailash Manasarovar** 1:200,000. Nepa Maps, Himalayan MapHouse; Paolo Gondoni.
- **From Lhasa to Kailas** 1:2,400,000. Nepa Maps, Himalayan MapHouse; Paolo Gondoni.
- **Nepal-Tibet** Namaste series, Pilgrims Book House; for the route to Lhasa and Far West Nepal.

Very few maps are available in Tibet. Lhasa is the only place where you might find anything.

In the UK one of the best places to search for maps of Tibet and the Himalayas is Stanfords on Long Acre in Central London; www.stanfords.co.uk. They stock a good selection of maps of the region.

Cho Oyu from the north (Qomolungma National Park)

PHOTOGRAPHY

Tibet and Nepal offer the keen photographer a wealth of interesting subject matter. People, buildings, scenery, markets, mountains and antiquities all add up to wonderful opportunities. The clarity of light on the Tibetan plateau is out of this world. But for the best results, remember:

- Keep all photographic equipment in plastic bags and away from heat/cold and dust whenever possible. You may need to sleep with your camera to keep it warm! Be particularly careful in the icy mornings, and ideally keep the camera tucked up close to your body inside a fleece to warm it up before use.
- Bring extra camera batteries and cleaning equipment. There will be few chances to recharge batteries for digital and video cameras, apart from Lhasa, Xigatse, Saga and Nyalam. It should also be possible in Darchen and Toling but electricity supplies can be erratic. Take a film camera as back-up.
- Buy all your film beforehand; although supplies are available in Kathmandu, you will not find any around Kailash.
- Do not take photographs of anything remotely military, such as checkposts, bridges, communication towers and border crossings.
- Do not take any photographs of people without first asking their permission.
- When flying, all films should be carried in hand luggage. Always check whether X-ray machines are safe for film; even if they say they are, it is safer to get your film hand-checked if possible.

Kailash, west face (Kailash Kora trek, Stage 2)

GETTING THERE

ROUTES INTO TIBET (VIA CHINA AND NEPAL)

Flights from China to Tibet

Air China has flights from Chengdu. Sichuan Airlines and Air China fly from Chengdu to Lhasa, with connections possible from other cities, for example Hong Kong, Chongqing, Xian, Kunming, Zhongdian, Xining and Kathmandu. Check with your local agent for up-to-date flight schedules, as they change frequently and with the seasons.

Overland from China

One overland route is from Golmud in Qinghai province, from where a new train service commenced on 1 July 2006. It is 4064km from Beijing to Lhasa, of which the last 1100km is on the new line across the Tibetan plateau. The train on this section is pressurised, with oxygen and air conditioning. Buses also run on this route; they take up to 36 hours and can be booked as part of a package to avoid bureaucratic problems.

Another land route recently opened to foreigners is from Chengdu and Zhongdian. Visitors can now arrange private jeeps and 4x4s with driver and guide to undertake this long arduous journey through the towns of Batang, Litang and Chamdo. The route traverses countless high ridges and crosses the upper gorges of the Yangtze, Mekong and Salween. It can take up to two weeks.

It is also possible to fly from Islamabad in Pakistan to Kashgar in Xinjiang province, but the difficulties of arranging transport and permits in Kashgar will preclude any visitors with a limited, fixed period of travel.

A very recent development is the agreed opening of the India/China border from Sikkim, but check beforehand, as it could involve special arrangements.

Flights to Kathmandu/Nepal

The main airlines operating to Kathmandu are:

- *Qatar Airways* via Doha
- *Gulf Air* via Bahrain or Abu Dhabi
- *Bangladesh Biman* via Dhaka
- *Thai Airways* via Bangkok
- *Nepal Airlines* from Delhi, Bombay, Dubai and Hong Kong
- *Druk Air* from Bhutan
- *Jet Airways* (India) a new service from London to Delhi with connections to Nepal
- *Air Sahara* (India) from Delhi to Kathmandu
- *Indian Airlines* from Delhi, Kolkata and Varanasi
- *Virgin* or *BA* direct to Delhi, and then with one of the Indian carriers to Kathmandu.

GMC Bangladesh, Korean Air and Air Arabia started services recently, and other airlines planning to fly to Nepal include *Orient Thai, Etihad Airways of United Arab Emirates (UAE)* and *Sri Lankan Airlines*.

This information is subject to change. With the peace agreement and new government, it is likely that many more airlines will start services, and other services may be reinstated.

KATHMANDU – GATEWAY TO TIBET

Kathmandu in Nepal is the most frequently used gateway to Kailash. The city abounds with interest, and its welcoming people make it a wonderful home away from home. There are numerous excellent hotels and guesthouses for all tastes. Myriad restaurants, cafés and pie shops provide varied and sustaining food; anything will be seen as sumptuous and delicious after two weeks in Tibet! Most tourists and trekkers will wish to spend a few extra days here to explore the city and its environs. Despite some modernisation, the valley holds some enchanting surprises.

At an altitude of 1317m, Kathmandu is a crossroads below the Himalayas; a trading centre and a melting pot of migrating peoples and religious ideas. The cities of Kathmandu, Patan, Bhaktapur and the surrounding valley host perhaps the greatest concentration of temples, shrines and idols anywhere in the world. The religious mingling of

Boudhanath stupa, Kathmandu

Patan Durbar Square Kathmandu valley

Hinduism, Buddhism, Tantra, Vajrayana, Tibetan Buddhism, Bon and Shamanism is a marvel in itself. Legends abound; tales, myths and folk stories are the lifeblood of Nepalese festivals and everyday life. The gods, goddesses and deities are the backbone of society. It is still fair to say that idols almost outnumber people, and temples outnumber tourists.

Kathmandu remains on the edge of the world, a treasure trove with a rich cultural heritage and still a valley of hidden enchantment. For a more

A DAY IN KATHMANDU

As dawn breaks, the dogs fall asleep but the city springs into life. It doesn't take long for the cacophony and chaos on the roads to build up. Pedestrians compete for space with bicycles, cycle rickshaws, motorbikes, motor rickshaws, taxis, buses and trucks on the vibrant colourful streets and alleys. But quiet corners, where little has changed for centuries, are still there to be found, with a few holy cows lingering close by. Hidden in the intricate maze of the narrow backstreets, potters still spin their wheels by hand and antique sewing machines perform miracles. Buddhists spin their prayer wheels as they walk, sending their prayers for peace skywards. And the dogs lie dormant, gaining strength for another night of action on the streets...

detailed appraisal of the valley's charms, see *Kathmandu: Valley of the Green-Eyed Yellow Idol* (Pilgrims).

What to see

No visit to Nepal would be complete without a thorough exploration of the **Durbar Squares** of the three great cities, **Kathmandu**, **Patan**, and **Bhaktapur**. In Kathmandu the central market area of Asan is a riot of colour. Close by, why not seek out the glittering courtyard temples of the **Seto** (White) **Machhendranath** in Jan Bahal? Buried within the lanes and alleys of the old city are **Itum Bahal**, **Sano** (little) **Swayambhunath** and the temple of **Nara Devi**.

Patan is a city of artisans and quiet quaint lanes. Deep in the old quarter are the **Kwa Bahal** (Golden Temple), the temple of the **Rato** (Red) **Machhendranath** and many other exquisite temples and shrines.

Bhaktapur, which lies 11km east, is the least modernised city of the valley. Its **Durbar Square** is intriguing. Don't miss its other squares: **Nyatapola**, with a five-tiered temple, and, to the east, **Dattatreya Square**, a majestic scene of intricately carved wooden windows and fine brick structures. In the quiet streets of Bhaktapur, time stands still. Its mediaeval atmosphere is a living relic of a forgotten era.

Not far beyond the valley ring road are some famous pilgrimage centres. On a hill to the west is the monkey temple, **Swayambhunath**, a picturesque Buddhist *stupa* surrounded by various shrines and temples. At

Bhaktapur Dattatreya Square, Kathmandu valley

Boudhanath to the east, Tibetan and Buddhist devotees circle the great *stupa*, seeking peace. Along the banks of the holy Bagmati river sits the temple complex of **Pashupatinath**, where Hindus offer their devotions to the deities, and where they are cremated before passage into the next life.

To the south of Patan lie some less visited shrines and villages. Foremost are **Bungamati** (Red Machhendranath temple and quaint houses), **Khokana** (Shekali Mai temple), **Pharping** (Buddhist monasteries and Guru Rinpoche cave), **Shesh Narayan** (a temple devoted to Vishnu) and **Dakshinkali** (an often gory temple, where pilgrims offer devotion and live sacrifices to the bloodthirsty goddess Kali).

Those with plenty of time can find other enchanting places that time has passed by. Places such as **Changu Narayan**, **Kirtipur**, **Vajra Yogini** near Sankhu, the boar-headed Vajra Varahi temple garden of **Chapagaon** and, further afield on a ridge, the mountain viewpoint of **Nagarkot**.

Accommodation

The tourist centre of Kathmandu, Thamel, is a backpacker's mecca, with restaurants and hotels to suit all pockets and appetites. Try the delightful Kathmandu Guest House (known as the KGH), always a lively place. Also here are the Hotels Garuda, Marshyangdi, Vaisali and Manang, and, a little further away, the quiet Norbu Linka. For a taste of Tibet, try the well run Hotel Tibet in Lazimpat; nearby is the comfortable and well managed Hotel Ambassador. Those seeking greater luxury can lodge at the Hotel Malla on the edge of Thamel, while further out are the Hotel Vajra, the Hotel Shankar, a former Rana palace, and the atmospheric heritage-style hotel of Dwarika's.

Eating out

There are too many restaurants to list them all. Exclusion from this list does not imply any criticism but we would advise caution when eating at cheaper places; indeed, choose your food particularly carefully before your trip to Tibet, as there is nothing worse than sitting in a car for hours on end suffering from Delhi-belly! Even in the better restaurants, we recommend you to avoid salads and unpeeled fruit as a precaution. Here is a selection of recommended places to eat: Pilgrims Feed 'n Read, Rum Doodle, Helena's, KC's, Yin Yang, Third Eye, Dechenling Garden, Kathmandu Guest House, New Orleans, North Field Café, Dolce Vita, Brezel Bakery, Le Bistro, Fire and Ice, Kilroy's and Mike's Breakfast (which serves lunch and dinner too). Moti Mahal in Durbar Marg serves delicious Indian food.

LHASA

For so long a forbidden city, modern Lhasa is rapidly changing. All the same, there remain pockets where the visitor can feel the great mystical draw

Potala, Lhasa, Tibet

of this former abode of the Buddhist God King, the Dalai Lama.

What to see

The major sight is of course the dominant **Potala Palace**, the former residence of the Dalai Lama. Is there a comparable structure to be found anywhere in the world? The first sight of this great colossus is simply stunning – a reminder of the mysterious enchantment of old Tibet. Below the Potala is the West Gate, the former entrance to the city, with its imposing *chortens* now rebuilt.

The Tibetan heart of the city is the **Jokhang Temple**, the spiritual centre of Tibet, where pilgrims come to pay homage to the Jowo image. Behind the Jokhang is the **Barkhor** area, a maze of alleyways and old buildings encircled by a street, a *kora* that serves as a colourful market and bazaar. The summer residence of the Dalai Lama, the **Norbulingka**, to the west is still a peaceful retreat.

The three great former monastic cities of Lhasa, **Drepung, Sera** and **Ganden** are impressive and still resonate with a spiritual atmosphere, despite the ravages of former times.

Accommodation

Today's traveller to Lhasa need not sneak into its byways looking for a kind soul to hide his presence, or even to hunt about for a cold guesthouse where the bedding hasn't been washed for decades, as the first independent tourists found in the mid-

Gyangtse, Tibet, including Palkor Choide stupa and Kumbum monastery (From Lhasa to Kailash (by road))

1980s. Today there is a good selection of hotels, guesthouses and lodges and one will surely not lack for nourishment any more.

From top of the range lodgings such as Lhasa Hotel, Tibet Hotel and Tibet International Grand Hotel, to budget/mid-range old favourites like the Snowlands, Banak Shol, Kirey and many others, there is no shortage of choice.

USING THIS GUIDE

Having whetted your appetite with some geographical, historical and cultural background, as well as perhaps dampened your enthusiasm over some of the less inspiring aspects of the journey – such as rooftop toilets – we come now to the trekking and travel section (see below).

The next three sections deal with the treks from Simikot to Kailash through western Nepal, the Kailash Kora trek itself, some brief notes on the walk around Lake Manasarovar and other shorter day hikes in the vicinity of Kailash. Getting to the mountain occupies a number of pages, because the journeys there and back are such an integral part of any expedition in Tibet.

The last section covers the ancient kingdom of Guge and the remains of the temples at Toling and Tsaparang. This is where the more significant cultural highlights are to be found. In order to enhance the descriptions, we have given a brief synopsis of the history behind the great monastic complexes. After this section there are some outline notes on visiting Everest North Base Camp.

A long list of books covering just about every facet of Tibet is included – enough material to satisfy the most ardent student of the culture – but not enough to make this book too heavy to carry over the Drolma La pass at 5660m!

NOTES ON TREKKING AND ROAD ROUTES

Altitudes, distances and timings

The descriptions of the trekking routes and the road routes include approximate distances, timings, altitudes and the gains or losses in height. Maps produced by different companies all give different distances and altitudes, so figures are approximate.

For driving routes, only the overall altitude gain for each stage is given. This is the figure that is important when considering acclimatisation.

Altitude gains and losses shown within the trekking descriptions attempt to indicate the actual changes along the walking trail. They cannot be definitive, given the lack of accuracy on any map and because different paths may be used by different parties, however they should give an indication of the amount of effort required.

Alternative names

Where place names, monasteries, mountains and deities have alternate names – in Sanskrit, Tibetan or Nepalese – the ones used in this guide are those in most common usage in the local area in question. Where it may be helpful to know them, alternative names have been provided in parentheses.

Kailash and Tarboche flagpole (Kailash Kora trek, Stage 1)

Milestones

Occasionally the routes refer to milestones (for example, Km5264). Milestones are numbered rectangular concrete blocks on the side of the road, indicating the distance from a particular place (often an unnamed crossroads in the middle of nowhere). In this context, they are included as landmarks and, when travelling between them, indications of distance travelled, rather than navigational aids.

Prices

Prices quoted in this guide, for accommodation and entrance fees to sites, are given in local currencies, as these remain relatively fixed, while exchange rates, particularly that of the US dollar, may fluctuate. Current exchange rates can be obtained from your bank, but see also 'Money matters' earlier.

APPROACH ROUTES TO KAILASH

Getting to the sacred mountain requires determination, reasonable health and for most people, a fair amount of money. It lies far from the Tibetan cities of Lhasa and Xigatse, far from any decent roads and a long way from what we might call civilisation.

One way is to trek in from **Simikot** in western Nepal. This option is sometimes restricted, although the situation changes frequently. Simikot is accessed by internal flights in Nepal via the Terai town of Nepalganj. The trek is a five or six day trip and, once across the border at Sher, a rough road climbs through Khojarnath (which has a monastery) to Purang (Taklakot). This trading town has a lively market in season, as well as various monastic ruins. The road climbs over the Gurla La pass on the western shoulder of Gurla Mandhata and descends to the two lakes, Manasarovar and Rakhas Tal. Kailash is just to the north.

Indian pilgrims also trek in from **the Indian border** slightly further west, travelling to Darchula by road and then trekking for eight to nine days before crossing the daunting Lipu Lekh pass and down to Purang. Foreigners are not currently permitted to follow this route.

Most westerners will come by road from **Kathmandu** or **Lhasa**. From Nepal it takes at least four days, travelling via Nyalam, Saga and Paryang. (On this route, you will cross the border at the Friendship Bridge, where your baggage will be sprayed with 'disinfectant', so make sure the contents are packed in plastic bags!) From Lhasa it may take a minimum of four long days, but allow five in your planning. There is also talk of an airport being built near Darchen, though this is likely to be some considerable time in the future, if at all.

Barkhor bazaar, Lhasa, Tibet

1 – From Simikot: the Trekking Route

Thanks to Pasang Dawa Sherpa of Sherpa Adventure Travel (see Appendix 6) for much of the following information. We were unable to do this trek ourselves, as the area was closed at the time of our visit and foreigners were not allowed on flights to Simikot.

This route is one way to aid acclimatisation, as the trek begins at about 2950m and climbs steadily to around 3800m at the border. However the sharp rise onto the plateau beyond Sher, on the drive up to Lake Manasarovar at 4550m, might still affect some people. There are currently virtually no lodges or teahouses on this trek, so all camping equipment and food must be sent in from Kathmandu. Fees are high due to logistical and local difficulties.

To reach Simikot in western Nepal, it is necessary to take an internal flight from Kathmandu. Currently no direct flights are offered, so you have to go via Nepalganj in the Terai lowlands of western Nepal. Currently this involves an overnight in Nepalganj, but there is one reasonable hotel, the Hotel Snehu. Remember to cover up around dusk and after dark, as this town lies in the **malaria risk** zone, and seriously consider taking antimalarial tablets. Malaria-carrying mosquitoes bite at this time of the day (see 'Health'). The flights to Nepalganj and on to Simikot offer tremendous views of the Himalayas, including Ganesh, Himalchuli, the Annapurnas, Dhaulagiri, Churen Himal, Kanjiroba, the western peaks of Api, Saipal, Nampur and, with luck, Gurla Mandhata. On arrival, most groups spend the rest of the day in Simikot (2950m), which sits high above the Karnali river.

STAGE 1:
Simikot to Tuling (Masigaon)

Altitude range	2950m to 2290m
Time	4–5hrs
Distance	8km
Altitude gain	250m
Altitude loss	910m
Highest point	3200m

After an initial ascent of around 250m from the Simikot airstrip, the trail is primarily downhill on this day. The route drops almost 1000m through forest into the deep and steep-sided canyon of the Karnali river. With few flat areas in this gorge, the settlements are small and quite poor. **Tuling**, a Thakuri village, is sometimes marked on maps as Masigaon (or Majgaon), its Nepali names. Groups often camp beyond the village at, or close to, the Yakba Khola.

STAGE 2:
Tuling to Kermi

Altitude range	2290m to 2670m
Time	4+hrs
Distance	9–10km
Altitude gain	500m
Altitude loss	120m
Highest point	2670m

Following the east bank of the Karnali river, the trail climbs steadily, crossing a couple of tributaries, the Hekpa Khola and the Talung Khola. These side valleys

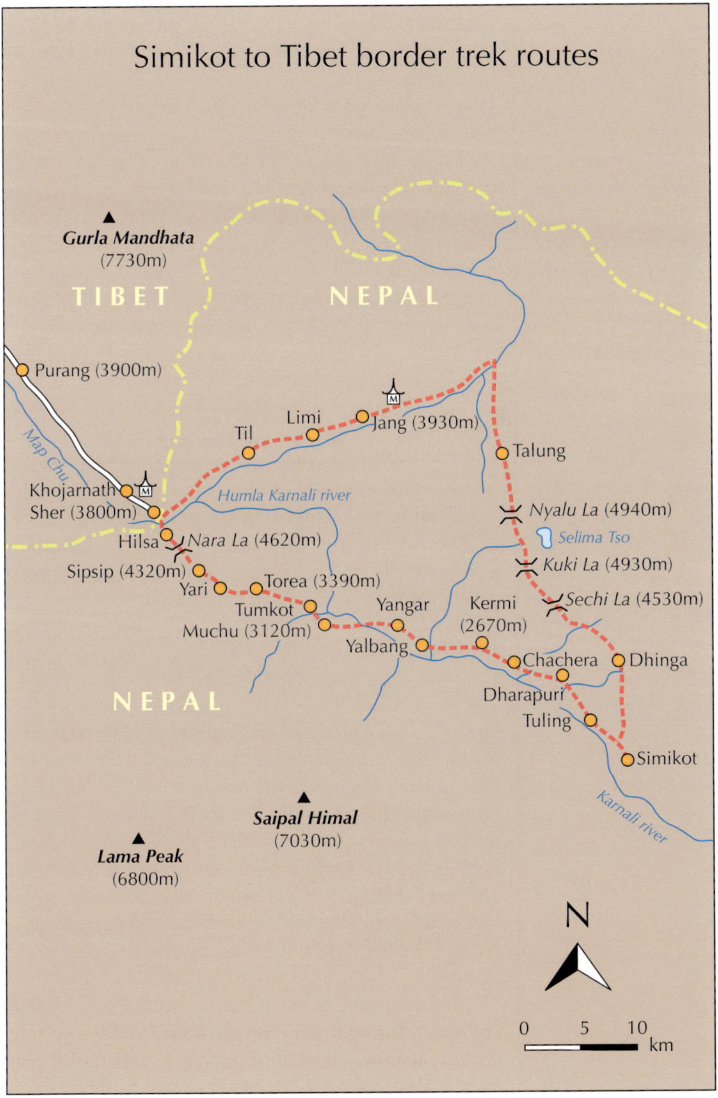
Simikot to Tibet border trek routes
Gurla Mandhata
(7730m)
TIBET
NEPAL
Purang (3900m)
Map Chu
Khojarnath
M
Sher (3800m)
Til
Limi
M
Jang (3930m)
Talung
Humla Karnali river
Hilsa
Nara La (4620m)
Nyalu La (4940m)
Selima Tso
Kuki La (4930m)
Sipsip (4320m)
Yari
Torea (3390m)
Tumkot
Yangar
Kermi
(2670m)
Sechi La (4530m)
Muchu (3120m)
Yalbang
Chachera
Dhinga
Dharapuri
NEPAL
Tuling
Simikot
Karnali river
Saipal Himal
(7030m)
Lama Peak
(6800m)
N
0
5
10
km

have some forests; the route has not yet reached the drier rain shadow region so typical of Tibet. The trekking is hard today, as the route has to climb up and descend steeply where parts of this sheer-sided gorge encroach and where difficult and dangerous sections of the valley floor have to be avoided. ◂ In a further 2hrs, the village of Kermi (2670m) is reached, although an optional trail also bypasses the settlement. With prayer flags and some *mani* walls about the village, Kermi is the first place that is inhabited by Tibetan people. There are a couple of monasteries above the village. One is a Sakya-pa *gompa* and the other is an older Nyingma-pa monastery.

The track passes through the small settlement of Dharapuri and on to Chachera, which has a waterfall and is a good lunch spot.

STAGE 3:
Kermi to Yangar

Altitude range	2670m to 3000m
Time	3–4hrs
Distance	10km
Altitude gain	410m
Altitude loss	80m
Highest point	3000m

This is a short day to aid acclimatisation, with time for a visit to the Kermi monasteries. Continuing along the Karnali river, the trail climbs up to around 3000m with occasional glimpses of the Saipal Himal peak. The path climbs into the side valley of the Chungsa Khola, crosses the river and then heads on to the village of **Yalbang**, noted for its apricot groves. There is a small monastery above the trail called Namka Khyung Zong, a Nyingma-pa *gompa* but with a distinctly Tibetan Bon name.

The afternoon is spent hiking along the riverbank and surmounting small ridges to **Yangar** village, where there is a health post set up by the Nepal Trust. An ancient trade route leads south from here.

STAGE 4:
Yangar to Muchu

Altitude range	3000m to 3120m
Time	4–5hrs
Distance	8km
Altitude gain	420m
Altitude loss	300m
Highest point	3150m

Today might look a short day on the map, but the nature of the terrain in the gorge of the Karnali ensures plenty of exercise, as the trail climbs and drops around obstacles in the valley. Sometimes the path clings to hillsides and in places pathways have been built out from the cliffs to give passage. Muchu stands at about 3120m, so there is little overall height gain.

STAGE 5:
Muchu to Yari

Altitude range	3120m to 3800m
Time	7–8hrs
Distance	10km
Altitude gain	780m
Altitude loss	100m
Highest point	3800m

Leaving Muchu and its monastery, the trail climbs to a ridge. Dropping into a ravine and climbing to a *chorten*, the path offers views of the Mota monastery of **Tumkot**, which is not on the main track. The trail now leaves the drama of the Karnali gorge, as the river diverts north into treacherous and impassable canyons. Trekkers must now climb arduously for over 2hrs to **Torea**, also called Palbang, at 3390m. Continuing up, the path eventually comes to **Yari**. Yari is a typical Bhotia-style village, with flat-roofed houses and a *gompa*. Most parties, however, continue on from Yari to the foot of the **Nara La** pass to camp.

STAGE 6:
Yari to Sher

Altitude range	3800m to 3800m
Time	4–5hrs
Distance	9km
Altitude gain	820m
Altitude loss	820m
Highest point	4620m

Today the route climbs to the village of **Sipsip** and on to the **Nara La** pass at 4620m, a climb that could well take 3hrs or more. ◂ The descent to **Hilsa** is steep, rough and knee-jarring – an 800m drop to the **Karnali river** and the border with Tibet.

The view from the pass is spectacular, with the closer peaks of Numuche, Kandamphu and Taku Himal to the north and the ramparts of Gurla Mandhata just visible far to the north-north-west.

Drive to Purang

Altitude range	3800m to 3900m
Time	2hrs
Distance	27km
Highest point	4000m

Sher is uphill on the Tibetan side of the river. From here visitors can drive to **Purang**, known as Taklakot by the Nepalese. En route is the Sakya-pa monastery of Khorja

(**Khojarnath**), which is of considerable antiquity and was founded by King Khor. The monastery site has links to the translator Rinchen Zangpo and is nearly 1000 years old. It takes about 2hrs to drive to Purang, a settlement with a strongly Chinese atmosphere. The trading settlement here is famed for its wool bazaars, caves and the Simbiling monastery that was heavily damaged in the late 1960s.

STAGE 7:
Purang to Lake Manasarovar/Darchen

Altitude range	3900m to 4550/4650m
Time	2–3hrs
Distance	80/100km
Altitude gain	650/750m
Highest point	approx 4700m

Before crossing the Gurla La pass (4700m), which is virtually on a shoulder of the peak of Gurla Mandhata, the road skirts a place called Toyo. ▶ From the pass the track descends to the lakes of Manasarovar and Rakhas Tal. A further 40min drive past the lakes takes you to the scruffy village of Darchen, at the foot of Kailash.

The Dogra Sikh scoundrel Zorawar Singh was killed here by the Tibetans after a long campaign from Jammu across Kinnaur, Spiti and Ladakh.

Alternative return trek route from Sher to Simikot

From the border a trail heads northeast to **Til**, **Limi** and the historic monastery at **Jang**. This trail can be used as an alternative for those returning to Simikot after the Kailash trip. It takes three days to trek to Jang from the border. This trail continues east and then south from Jang, through **Talung** and over the **Nyalu La** pass at 4940m. Two further passes are crossed – the **Kuki La** (4930m) and the **Sechi La** (4530m), which appears as the Landok Lagna on some maps. The settlement of **Dhinga** is the last place before meeting the main trail near **Tuling** and turning south into Simikot. This trek from Sher to Simikot takes seven days.

2 – FROM KATHMANDU TO KAILASH (DARCHEN) (BY ROAD)

Kathmandu to Kodari

Altitude range	1317m to 2300m
Time	5hrs
Distance	114km
Altitude gain	980m
Highest point	2300m

This is an exceptionally scenic drive in clear weather, with the Himalayan chain displayed in all its grandeur to the north. A long line of shimmering white peaks stretches to an infinite horizon in both directions.

Nepal, Himalayas from Dhulikhel

The road to Kodari, the town just on the Nepalese side of the Tibetan border, is quite fast for much of its length, but deteriorates considerably about 1 hr from the border. The whole journey will take about 4–5hrs, and along the way you can stop at Dhulikhel for lunch, enjoying scenic views of the Himalayan chain from the restaurant terrace. Arriving at Kodari, a scruffy border town that looks as though it is about to fall into the river gorge, you may wish to get away quickly. But if you have the time and energy, a night at the Eco Resort just 15mins walk uphill before the town is recommended. Here you can get your last taste of luxury, in the form of en suite hot showers and toilets you can sit on, as well as good food. It also has the advantage of being higher than the town and certainly much higher than Kathmandu, assisting in acclimatisation. This is particularly important when driving to Tibet, as there is no easy way out if you should become ill.

Accommodation

Eco Resort $50 double en suite with dinner. The hotel will arrange porters to carry your baggage.

Other scruffy guesthouses in the town are only worth considering if you're on a very tight budget (in which case you are unlikely to be going to Kailash anyway!) or don't have the energy for a 15min walk up a steep hill to the Eco Resort.

Kodari/Zhangmu to Nyalam

Altitude range	2300m to 3750m
Time	1hr
Distance	33km
Altitude gain	1350m
Highest point	3750m

The drive almost vertically upwards to Nyalam must be one of the fastest road ascents in the world, and is, without doubt, breathtaking in both senses of the word.

There will be some bureaucracy to sort out at the border, but all should be in order if you are travelling with a local guide. ◂ Cross the border at the Friendship Bridge. This is a time-consuming activity. You will need to be met by the tour operator who has arranged your visa. Then you will probably have tea while they sort out the rest of the paperwork. The border town of **Zhangmu** is a hive of activity; trucks line the narrow streets and there are often long traffic jams, as the road is just too narrow for trucks to pass. Nepalese trucks bring their cargo from Nepal, but it must all be transferred to Chinese trucks to continue its journey on to the Tibetan plateau.

From Zhangmu the road climbs steeply up through an impressive gorge; in only 1hr you will be in **Nyalam**, at 3750m – a tremendous change in altitude and one that requires rest and lots of cups of tea. Nyalam still has one old Tibetan street, but the rest of the town consists mostly of ugly Chinese structures. For those with time or taking a day to aid acclimatisation, there are fine hikes in the Nyanang valley west of Nyalam. See 'Xixapangma Trekking Routes' below.

Phurbi Chyachu peak from the Tibetan side, near Nyalam

Accommodation

Various 50 Yuan for a double

A selection of fairly basic guesthouses can be found in the main street. These offer multi-bedded rooms with toilets of the squat variety outside, and, as usual in China, with low or no partitions between the row of holes in the floor. You will be provided with a flask of hot water, china cups and a large bowl.

Eating out

Try at the guesthouses; food is basic but acceptable.

Xixapangma trekking routes

Xixapangma (also written Shishapangma, and known as Gosainthan by the Nepalese) at 8012m is the highest mountain completely within the Tibetan region. One of the most inaccessible mountains in the world, it was first climbed by a Chinese team in 1964. Once the Nepal–Tibet border opened, mountaineers flocked to challenge its summits. In 1982 Doug Scott and the late Alex MacIntyre climbed the mountain from its southern side.

Seen from Nepal, the mountain hides behind the mass of peaks of the Jugal Himal, but viewed from its northern flanks, it and the satellite peak Phola Gangchen utterly dominate the plains. From the Lalung La pass, its grandeur cannot be denied.

There are three approaches to the mountain. The approach through the eastern valley – a narrow, almost hidden, route – is little used. The north side is easily accessed from Km5264 on the Nyalam to Tingri highway and later via Siling village. About 15km south of Siling, there is a campsite which affords shelter from icy winds and offers spectacular views of the entire range of Phola Gangchen, Xixapangma, Gangphu Ri Shah through to Lalaga Ri in the west. The two-day trek from here into base

Xixapangma trekking routes
to Saga
TIBET
Pekhu Tso
Siling
Lalung La pass
Lalaga Ri
Gangphu Ri
Milarepa Cave
Monastery
Langtang Ri
Phola Gangchen
Xixapangma
Nyanang Ri
Chobo
Bamare
Kyungka Ri
Pemthang
Karpo Ri
Nyanang Chu
Lenpogang
Nyalam
Tara Tso
Langtang
Dorje Lakpa
Phurbi Chyachu
NEPAL
Zhangmu
Kodari
to Kathmandu
N
0
5
10
km

camp at 4900m and is virtually flat, with imperceptible increases in altitude. The third option, the southern route, is the most commonly used passage from Nyalam, a two-day hike one way.

Xixapangma south approach

For those with **at least one full day** to acclimatise and enough energy, the trek towards the south Xixapangma base camp is full of dramatic mountain views and tranquil scenes backed by tremendous icy vistas. The trek offers close-up views of the Nepalese Jugal Himal peaks, the peaks of the upper Langtang valley of Nepal and the southern ramparts of Xixapangma. Note that these treks are very high early in a trip and it would be preferable to have walked high in Nepal first if you can make time on your itinerary.

Nyalam to Tara Tso day hike

Time	6–7hrs
Distance	12–14km
Altitude gain	500m
Altitude loss	500m
Highest point	4250m

From **Nyalam**, head initially up to the monastery at the top of the old quarter of town. A path from here heads west across what remains of fields. There is a well-defined track that edges towards some stone buildings below the hillside immediately west of town. It takes about 1hr to reach this area. Yak herders (and dogs) congregate here. The Nyanang Chu valley narrows as the river to the right cuts its way around a bend. Once around this bend, it widens out to reveal distant peaks. Distances in this valley are very deceptive, and it would

Xixapangma north, campsite

take a full two days to reach what is considered to be the south base camp. The best option for this acclimatising hike is to climb one of the two ridges that ascend from the river. The ridge further west is the better option, for it reveals a beautiful lake, **Tara Tso**, on the plateau shelf, perhaps 500m up from the valley.

Since it is always recommended to climb high and sleep low, this trek makes an ideal acclimatisation day walk before heading on to Saga and Kailash.

From here a wonderful panorama unfolds, with the south faces of Xixapangma on view. To the south is the north face of Phurbi Chyachu, and to the west are Dorje Lakpa, Lenpogang and Pemthang Karpo Ri. The estimated height of the lake here is about 4300m and the walk might take 3 hrs from Nyalam. ◂ Going all the way to the south base camp area would be a good warm-up trek of three or four days. It would add considerably to the cost of an organised trip.

Nyalam to Saga

Altitude range	3750m to 4280m
Time	8–9hrs
Distance	252km
Altitude gain	530m
Highest point	c5000m

This is a long day, but what a day! Soon after leaving Nyalam, you reach the site of the **Milarepa Cave** where Milarepa meditated, and where a Kagyu-pa **monastery** has now been built. Entry costs 10 Yuan. The road climbs up further to cross the Lalung La pass (4910m), with stunning views of the Himalayan peaks, in particular Phurbi Chyachu, Dorje Lakpa, Gauri Shankar, Menlungtse and the snowy realms of Xixapangma. Soon after this viewpoint, a small track marked 'no cars' leads off to the left. This becomes a fairly wide route across a flattish plain, in the direction of Xixapangma. It is about 1hr 30mins to the valley of Xixapangma, with a camping

Xixapangma massif from Lalung La pass

Tibetan woman and child in Siling village, Xixapangma north

spot below the low plateau cliff. This route goes south of **Siling** (Serlung), past a checkpost and entrance to the Xixapangma National Reserve.

There is a very primitive guesthouse 4–5hrs from Nyalam on the southern shore of Pekhu Tso (4595m), the only one on this route. This is a basic building; there are no toilets. The beds are not level. Furthermore, the altitude is extremely dangerous for those who have just come from Kathmandu, so do not linger here any longer than necessary. On the northeastern shores of Pekhu Tso is the Bon Palha Phuk hermitage. Bon call the lake Pal Khyung Tso. There are some paintings here, as well as a Bon mantra on a rock at the village entrance.

If you stay at Pekhu Tso the day's height gain is 850m, which is extremely dangerous.

It's a long drive of 3–4hrs to Saga, but since Saga is at only 4280m, it is well worth continuing. ◂ Dropping down 300m will help to reduce the almost inevitable headaches and other symptoms of altitude sickness. The road heads around the lake, up to a small pass and goes down north along the ridge top. After a settlement the road improves briefly, crossing a pass before dropping to the shores of a soda lake. After two higher passes, the track descends steeply towards the Tsangpo river. There

Our vehicle near Pekhu Tso

is a new bridge here crossing the river where the road goes east into the modern Chinese town of Saga. Tibetan quarters can be found to the north and also to the south. Saga is at Km1846.

Accommodation

Moon Star Hotel 150 Yuan double with hot shower; although these do not always work, this hotel is currently the only chance you'll get to enjoy this sort of luxury! The food is also excellent.

Yiangje Yiange 45 Yuan per bed; in the Tibetan quarter.

New hotels opposite the Moon Star.

There are also some cheaper Tibetan hotels with very primitive facilities.

Telephone calls can be made from various shops around town.

Eating out

The Moon Star is good.

A SAGA IN SAGA

Amidst swirling snowflakes and threatening clouds, we pulled into the town of Saga. The first choice for accommodation suggested by our guide was a Tibetan-style guesthouse with a toilet at least 50m from the room, outside across the sub-zero dark and icy courtyard. Given the impending storm, this did not appeal, despite our preference for all things Tibetan. Our heads too felt distinctly unappealing, swimming from an excess of high altitude after crossing three passes.

The Moon Star Hotel, a Chinese concrete box, proved to be our temporary Shangri-la, with a draughty sliding panoramic window that didn't fit. So cold was our room that we needed to stand under the infrared lamps in our private 'bathroom' to feel remotely warm. At least the Chinese have brought inside toilets to Tibet!

All night a blizzard cast doom over our mood. Could any high pass be open after such an arctic embrace? We spent most of the next day in bed, trying to keep warm and nursing slightly sore heads. Was this Shangri-la, watching Chinese and Mongolian B-class movies? The satellite TV service provided an almost infinite number of channels, but all were in Chinese, with the exception of perhaps one or two in Tibetan. Dreams of Kailash seemed far away...

After 37 hours in infrared 'paradise', we were only too pleased the next morning to slip and slide our way over a frozen wasteland to the land of dreamers.

Saga to Paryang

Altitude range	4280m to 4610m
Time	8hrs
Distance	252km
Altitude gain	330m
Highest point	5100m

This is a day of contrasts. The excitement mounts as you get ever closer to the sacred peak. Along the way, the white line of the Himalayas stretches out as far as the eye can see. Add sand dunes, a beautiful lake and a fascinating monastery, and you have all the ingredients for a perfect day.

Leaving Saga, the road climbs gently to the north and crosses a small pass. It is then relatively flat, below towering peaks to the north and lower ranges to the south. After the settlement of Lhatsekhang, the road surface is generally good. There are some fort-like ruins and a monastery to the north on a high hillside. It takes around 3hrs 30mins to the village of Drongba (also sometimes written as Drongpa), which has a couple of guesthouses and restaurants.

DRONGBA MONASTERY

The *gompa* here is called the Monastery of the Seven Hairs. It belongs to the Sakya-pa, hence the grey walls, and contains some striking figures. The main sanctum has a colossal statue of Guru Rinpoche, indicating the presence of the Nyingma-pa here in earlier times. The guardian deities of the chapel are four equally impressive figures, including Tamdrin and Vajrapani. A close inspection near the doors will reveal an intriguing picture of the two-headed bird on a mural, which can be seen in two ways at once.

Siân at Drongba monastery

Leaving Drongba, the road crosses a broad flat region with rivers and plains, and then follows the blue waters of the Tsangpo for a while. The foothills of the isolated, formerly independent, kingdom of Mustang are just to the south in Nepal. The high snowy peak of Mansail, a mountain visible from Lo Manthang on the Nepalese side, is in view. On a very clear day you can just make out the Nepalese mountains of Tilicho, the cluster of the Annapurna peaks and Dhaulagiri a long way south.

There are some dramatic sand dunes after this, particularly when snow-covered. On the approach to Paryang the valley widens out again into open plains. Herds of yak graze on these golden plains; behind them you should have clear mountain views of the peaks of Upper Dolpo, including perhaps Kanjiroba. The drive from Drongba to Paryang takes around 2hrs 30 mins.

On arrival in Paryang, there are three guesthouses and a huge pile of yak dung in the centre. At the market you can bargain for purses and other knick-knacks, photograph the nomads who have come into town (asking permission first) and see their colourful tents. There is also a monastery close to the centre of the village and a small clinic and pharmacy.

Sand dunes on the banks of theTsangpo river near Drongba

Accommodation

Yak Hotel 50 Yuan per bed. The rooftop toilet at the Tibetan Yak Hotel, in a nice courtyard, has a view without comparison. For ladies who don't squat too low, the entire Himalayan chain is there on stage before your eyes as you contemplate. Tall men should be discreet, as the ladies have the front row of the theatre... There are three parallel holes for women and the same for men, with only a low wall separating the two sexes. The mother and daughter who run the place have some of the best examples of Tibetan turquoise headdresses you are likely to see anywhere.

Tashi Guesthouse A Tibetan-style guesthouse, very similar standard to the Yak (including the toilets).

Office Hotel A Chinese-style hotel.

Eating out

Try the Chinese food at Tianfu or the Chongqing.

Paryang to Lake Manasarovar/ Chui Gompa

Altitude range	4610m to 4550m
Time	7hrs
Distance	250km plus 15km to lakeside
Altitude loss	460m
Highest point	5140m

This is not a particularly long day, but with so much to see, there will be a lot of photo-stops. Today offers the first views of the sacred peak of Kailash, standing supreme above a golden plain.

Drokpa nomad tents

From Paryang the route continues across wide, open plains, but some low hills temporarily block the views to the south later. The road crosses some small passes; one pass is quite steep on its approach, as is the descent. Near Satsam there is an isolated building offering basic noodles for lunch. After this it is on to the Maryum La (5140m), around 120km from Paryang. It's not a difficult pass and is not steep. The view from here is not particularly impressive, but later on, as the route emerges from low hills, some massive peaks come into view to the southwest; this is northwestern Nepal.

About 2hrs from lunch, after the Maryum La, you pass the small but very blue Gung Gyo Gulmo; this is one of four revered Bon lakes of Shangshung.

Shortly after this, just before the village of Hor, is the first view of the sacred mountain you have come so far to see. The spot is marked by a large collection of prayer flags inside a stone circle, which you might wish to walk slowly around in a clockwise direction, while taking in the monumental significance of actually getting to this point!

To the south is the massive hulk of Gurla Mandhata (7730m), also known as Namo Nanyi by Tibetans. The

Prayer flags at the first view of Kailash on the eastern approach

turnoff for Lake Manasarovar is about 15km further west. Here various tracks head south to Chui Gompa and beyond, to the Gurla La pass and Taklakot on the road to Nepal.

The village below the Chui monastery on the west side overlooks the Ganga Chu river, which now flows between the two lakes of Manasarovar and Rakhas Tal. It appears saline and dirty, but there is a 'hot spring shower' room below the village.

Accommodation

Chui guesthouse 25–45 Yuan per bed. The only guesthouse has a cosy restaurant, but the outside loo, shared with the entire local community, is somewhat abominable, despite its incomparable view of Kailash. It is also rather unsafe, being made of rotten wood and perched above the cliff almost falling into the river. Keep your legs crossed as well as your fingers if you are contemplating using these facilities!

Chui village and Kailash

Lake Manasarovar to Darchen

From Chui monastery a rough track heads north for about 15km to the main road. A further 15km west is the Darchen turnoff, where your road again goes north.

3 – FROM LHASA TO KAILASH (BY ROAD)

This long drive will take four to five days (see overview map of The Himalayan Region). There are three roads between **Lhasa** and **Xigatse**: a northern route over high passes, a new road along the Tsangpo river, and the traditional southern route. The latter is the most interesting. It goes via **Yamdrok Tso**, a stunningly beautiful deep turquoise lake below the peaks of the Karo La, and

Kailash and Darchen village

through the fascinating traditional small town of **Gyangtse**. Gyangtse is home to the famous Palkor Choide *stupa* and monastic complex, as well as the famous Dzong, the fort that resisted the Younghusband campaign.

From Xigatse the road heads west to **Lhatse** and then through spectacular gorges below jagged ranges via **Raka** to **Saga**. From Saga it is two further days' drive to **Lake Manasarovar**. A minimum of four days is required, but five would make the journey much more relaxing and enjoyable, with time to appreciate the exceptional historical and cultural sites along the way.

THE KAILASH KORA TREK

We shall not cease from exploration
And the end of all our exploring
Will be to arrive where we started
And know the place for the first time

Four Quartets T S Eliot.

Hindu visitors refer to the Kailash Kora circuit walk as the Kailash Parikrama. There are four spots where Tibetan pilgrims prostrate to the mountain; these are called the four *chaktsel gang* (devotional spots). At three sites there are images on rocks, which are reputedly places where Buddha left his footprints. These are known as the *shabje*. All around the circuit are prayer flags at auspicious points. These multicoloured flags offer pilgrims' prayers and devotion to the deities as they flutter in the wind. Many of the flags have the symbol of the 'wind horse' on them, meaning move the 'spiritual breath' that blows with the wind to cleanse the soul.

Many of the peaks and ridges have the names of different deities. The Tibetan names are given first, with the better-known Sanskrit names shown in brackets.

Nomad tent in Lha Chu valley

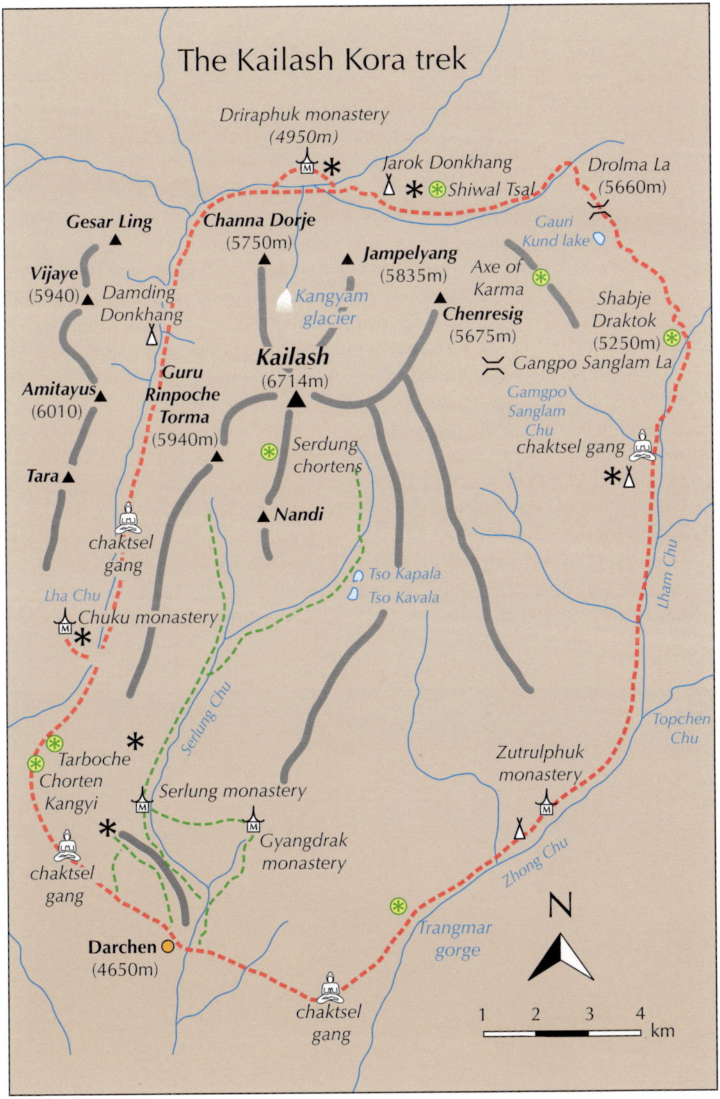
The Kailash Kora trek
Driraphuk monastery
(4950m)
Jarok Donkhang
Shiwal Tsal
Drolma La
(5660m)
Gesar Ling
Channa Dorje
(5750m)
Gauri
Kund lake
Jampelyang
(5835m)
Axe of
Karma
Vijaye
(5940)
Damding
Donkhang
Kangyam
glacier
Chenresig
(5675m)
Shabje
Draktok
(5250m)
Kailash
(6714m)
Gangpo Sanglam La
Guru
Rinpoche
Torma
(5940m)
Amitayus
(6010)
Gamgpo
Sanglam
Chu
Serdung
chortens
chaktsel gang
Tara
Nandi
chaktsel
gang
Tso Kapala
Tso Kavala
Lham Chu
Lha Chu
Chuku monastery
Serlung Chu
Topchen
Chu
Tarboche
Chorten
Kangyi
Zutrulphuk
monastery
Serlung monastery
Gyangdrak
monastery
chaktsel
gang
Zhong Chu
Darchen
(4650m)
Trangmar
gorge
N
chaktsel
gang
1 2 3 4 km

Darchen

Darchen (4650m) is the trailhead for the Kailash Kora trek for all visitors. It is a rapidly expanding village, set below a ridge festooned with prayer flags. The name Darchen means 'place of the large prayer flag' and the river it partially straddles comes from the Kailash Inner Kora valleys. This river flows south to Lake Rakhas Tal. In Darchen there is a monastery called Drukpa Gompa. At the northern end of the village a new Swiss-financed monastic museum and clinic have been completed. A *chorten* and *mani* wall close to the new clinic complex serve as the start and finish of the Kora.

Accommodation

The number of rooms available is increasing, but standards are generally very basic.

Tibet Manasarovar Travels Guesthouse Doubles/triples, 120–150 Yuan per person

Yak Hotel Near the *chorten*, dormitory beds, 25–45 Yuan per person

Kailash and the Lha Chu valley from the south

Government Guesthouse (Kangtise Hotel) Double room, 250 Yuan
Indian pilgrims have access to dormitory-style rooms in Darchen. Foreign visitors will probably be housed in the places listed above. Many visitors favour camping in season, but don't expect flat, soft pasture close to the village.

Eating out

There are a number of small restaurants north of the Tibet Manasarovar Travels guesthouse that are within local houses. None offer gourmet delights. Stick to pot noodles and black tea, especially before the trek!

Darchen monastery/ cultural centre

Our porters

Porters and yaks

In season yaks and porters can be in great demand, so forward planning is essential. Our two porters each cost 280 Yuan for the two and a half days. Yaks, which carry the equivalent of two porters, are around 150 Yuan per day and, with the yak manager, cost about 200–220 Yuan in total a day. Porters and yak managers appreciate tips for their services.

Other information

Some individual visitors have been required to obtain a permit for the Kora from the Public Security Bureau. The cost is 50 Yuan. For group visitors or those with Tibetan crews, any fees should be included in the package.

NB: The following stages do not necessarily represent day treks between campsites or overnight stops. (See Appendix 3 for suggested day stages.)

STAGE 1:
Darchen to Chuku monastery

Altitude range	4650m to 4810m
Time	3–4hrs
Distance	9km
Altitude gain	260m
Altitude loss	100m
Highest point	4810m

The trek begins in **Darchen** at the *chorten* and *mani* wall at the northern edge of the village. The obvious trail from hre heads west along the base of the ridge that obscures Kailash from view. Within 15 mins of leaving Darchen, you see the first prayer wheels. Turn these (clockwise) and send a prayer for a safe, rewarding trek. There are some small gullies on the right carving up the hillside. This path can be quite dusty, particularly when the wind is strong.

Tarboche prayer flags

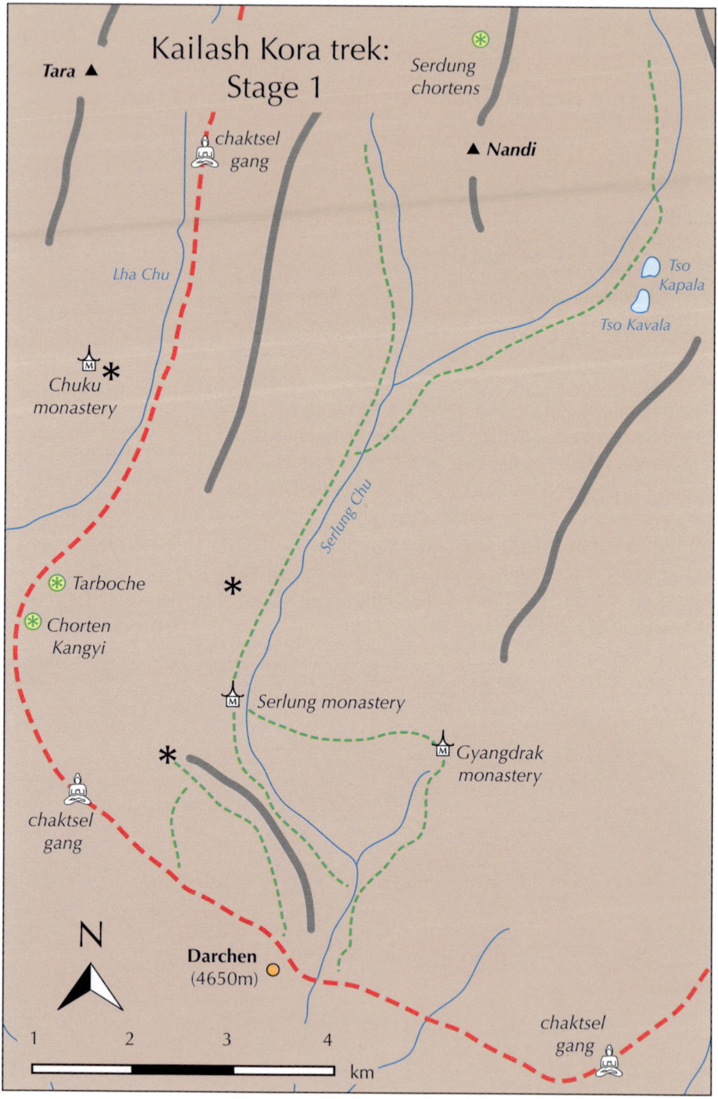
Kailash Kora trek:
Stage 1
Tara
Serdung
chortens
chaktsel
gang
Nandi
Lha Chu
Tso
Kapala
Tso Kavala
Chuku
monastery
Serlung Chu
Tarboche
Chorten
Kangyi
Serlung monastery
Gyangdrak
monastery
chaktsel
gang
N
Darchen
(4650m)
1
2
3
4
km
chaktsel
gang

After a wide, steeply rising valley to the right and some rest houses below the path, the trail climbs steadily but not steeply to the first *chaktsel gang*. The site is marked by stones, some covered with texts, cairns and prayer flags. This point is about 4km from Darchen and takes between 1.5hrs and 2hrs to reach. To the south, given clear skies, the great mass of Gurla Mandhata and the Nepalese peaks of Api, Saipal and Nampur rise dramatically.

From here the Kora trail turns north into the amazing and forbidding dark canyon of the **Lha Chu**, which means 'divine river'. Soon the first view of Kailash comes into sight, peeping above the canyon walls. This western valley is known as the canyon of Amitabha, the red Buddha of the west. If you started very early from Darchen it is likely that this initial walk into the canyon will be bitterly cold. The trail, which is generally easy underfoot, descends very gently for an hour or so to **Tarboche**.

▸ The summit of Kailash towers above to the northeast, a great cone of ice and rock. Notice the rugged grandeur of the western wall of the canyon here; its reddish walls may well be a gorgeous bright pink as the sun rises. The Tarboche flagpole is replaced each year during the spring Saga Dawa festival, which occurs on the full moon in May (or sometimes in June). This festival celebrates the enlightenment of the Buddha. (See 'Festivals'.)

The significant feature of Tarboche is a tall, graceful flagpole. It is festooned, like a maypole, with hundreds of prayer flags.

To the right or northeast of the pole is the raised plateau-like platform of the burial grounds known as Drachom Ngagye Durtro. Few trekkers will visit this holy

Profile 1: Darchen to Chuku monastery

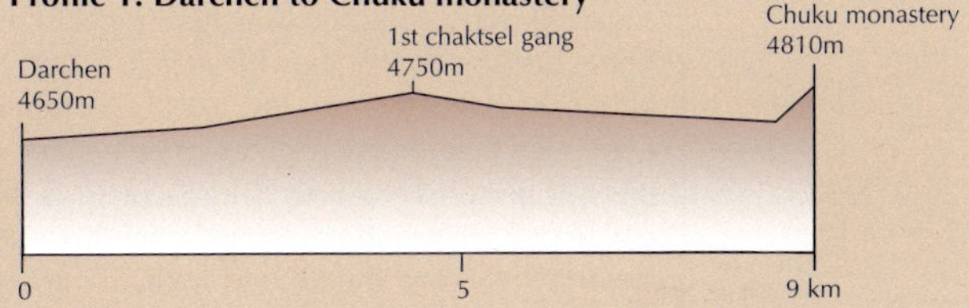

Siân in the Lha Chu valley

but sombre plinth, as this is the place of the dead. It is the haunt of the 84 Mahasiddhas, those mystic Tantric saints who have reached a higher insight or awareness. These burial grounds are where *lamas*, sages and saints have passed into the next life. Sky burials are sometimes performed here. Many pilgrims come up here to leave a piece of personal clothing, hair or a piece of their fingernail in order to gain merit for their rebirth. Countless personal items cover the ground here. Some outcrops of rock serve as sacred altars.

A cave near the burial ground was used by the Bon magician Naro Bonchung in which to meditate. There is reputed to be a footprint of Milarepa above the cave opening. According to Tibetan mythology, Naro Bonchung and the Buddhist saint Milarepa, who fought each other for control of Kailash, engaged in one of their duels here. A small stream close by drains into the main **Lha Chu** river and is called the Tshechu, or water of longevity. Pilgrims may be seen here placing its waters on their heads three times. Just to the left of the cave is a bowl-shaped rock known to pilgrims as the Tshokzhung. It is considered to be a sacred pot used by the spirits.

Close to Tarboche is the **Chorten Kangyi** (also spelt Kangnyi), an archway that theoretically marks the beginning of the Kora. It is considered auspicious to pass under this or pass it on the left. Note the symbolic moon and sun on the top of the *chorten*. These signs help to purify the pilgrims against bad karma – the negative effects of one's personal actions. A rough dirt track to this point is sometimes used by motor vehicles that carry ailing or disabled pilgrims, and some weary trekkers in order to shorten the walk!

From the *chorten* the path crosses a wide-open area known as Sershung, or 'pot of gold', because of an ancient legend. The trail is easygoing, allowing time to admire the defile ahead. It is now that the valley narrows, with the imposing ghost-like walls of the canyon looming overhead. This is the lair of the gods and it feels like it! The walls of the canyon on the Kailash side are surprisingly smooth, with fascinating forms. After passing the almost indistinct remnants of some *chortens* and *mani* walls, a solitary stone building is reached, no more than an hour from Tarboche.

Close to the building is the bridge that gives access across the Lha Chu to the path leading up to Chuku monastery (4810m). The monastery clings to the face of the cliffs of the Nyenri mountain, which is considered to be the abode of the Buddhist protector of the Kailash region, Kangri Lhatsen. The monastery is sometimes referred to as the Nyenri Gompa. It takes about 25mins

Kailash from the southwest, Lha Chu valley

to climb up the rough stony track to reach it. **Take care here**, as some of the rocks are unstable and at this altitude your concentration and climbing skills are apt to be below par. Belonging to the Kagyu-pa sect, this monastery was founded in the 13th century by a sage called Gotsangpo, who is credited with being the discoverer of the Kora route.

Inside the monastery, the main object of interest is a marble statue known as Chuku Rinpoche. The origin of this gem is shrouded in legends; one suggests it came from a sacred lake across the Himalayas in the Spiti-Lahaul region of northern India. Two other venerated objects, which may also have come from India, are a conch shell with a silver lining, called Chodung Thongwa Kundrol, and a copper vessel. The conch shell is said to remove bad karma. For Tibetan pilgrims, these three items represent the body, speech and mind of the Buddha.

A cave in the back of the monastery is the meditation place of Gotsangpo, who was born in the latter part of the 12th century. Another cave nearby is said to have been used by Milarepa (See Appendix 2). Much harder to find nearby is yet another cave known as the Elephant

Cave, in which the Tantric master Padma Sambhava meditated. The eponymous elephant's tusks are apparently sometimes displayed in the chapel of the Chuku monastery.

Across the valley from here there are considered to be 16 *arhats*, who are revealed in the rocks of the cliff face almost opposite and to the north of Chuku monastery. An *arhat* is a being who has divorced himself or herself from the cycle of life or existence. Only well-informed pilgrims are likely to appreciate these mythical figures. The views from Chuku monastery are amazing, with Kailash dwarfing the canyon from here.

STAGE 2: *Chuku monastery to Driraphuk monastery*

Altitude range	4810m to 4950m
Time	4–5hrs
Distance	11km
Altitude gain	220m
Altitude loss	80m
Highest point	4950m

On returning to the valley floor of the Lha Chu, there is a choice of routes. The traditional Kora trail follows the east bank, which passes below the now familiar forbidding cliffs. On the west bank the trail offers slightly better views of Kailash at times, but there are extra rivers to cross later. The west bank also offers camping parties some pristine grassy meadows 2hrs further north, in an area known as Damding Donkhang (4880m). Our description follows the traditional east bank.

The east bank trail now undulates gently on, although it may not seem so gentle on the short inclines. To the right are stupendous cliffs, the western buttresses of Kailash. An occasional gully or canyon tempts with

Damding Donkhang, nomad tent

tantalising views of the mountain's sheer west face. The trail is very clear and well worn along here. On the left or west side of the main valley are the three peaks that represent the three Bodhisattvas (Buddhist disciples) of longevity. From south to north they are called Drolma (**Tara**), a female deity who has 21 incarnations, Tsepame (**Amitayus**), an aspect of Amitabha, the west-facing Dhyani Buddha, and Namgyal-ma (**Vijaye**), a female deity whose name means victory. A few small streams cascade down from these crags, although they are often frozen into snakes of ice.

With the sun illuminating the valley, this stretch from Chuku to Damding Donkhang (4880m) becomes a peaceful and pleasant walk, unless there is a bitter wind blowing. Along the way, look out for the **rock of the 21 Taras** (Drolma Nyishu Tsakchik in Tibetan), which has many inscriptions. There is also a second prostration point, or *chaktsel gang* near here. The trail continues to be easy underfoot, allowing time to admire the views. On the east side of the canyon is a squat, craggy outcrop known as the **Guru Rinpoche Torma** (its Tibetan name is Tyupunjung). Hindus consider this ghost-shaped pile a vision of Hanuman the monkey god, associated with Rama.

With thoughts of refreshment not far ahead, the trekker may begin to radiate with renewed spiritual awakening in the warm sun. Along this section of the walk, given clear skies, you should enjoy truly spectacular views of Kailash. The west face towers improbably high above, with its dark striated horizontal layers clearly displayed. Very likely a plume of spindrift will be blowing from its icy summit above these demonic ramparts. However, photographers may find the sun streaming into their lenses, making picture-bagging problematic. Close to Damding Donkhang on the east bank, about two hours from the Chuku monastery bridge, several nomad tents offer physical sustenance in season to weary pilgrims and hikers. These tented teahouses remain pitched here throughout the pilgrimage season, from May to the end of October.

For those camping, the meadow area of Damding Donkhang is about 6 to 7hrs walk from Darchen. The name Damding is derived from Tamdrin, the fearsome Buddhist protector.

Continuing on up the valley, the walls of the canyon become less hostile. On the west side they retreat a little, offering wider vistas of rugged peaks. A couple of side valleys are seen to the west after the nomad tents, beyond a peak north of Vijaye called **Gesar Ling**. These are drained by the Belung Chu and, a little further on, by the Dunglung Chu from the north. To the east the mood changes again, as the westerly ramparts of the north face of Kailash begin to appear. The Kora trail follows the main valley, which becomes broader where it swings to the northeast. Grassy spots are a delight along the banks of the river, which is braided here and there. Kailash is lost to view as the path climbs more steadily towards the monastery of **Driraphuk** (Diraphuk). This stretch seems to take much more effort and you start to wonder why, until you look behind you and realise how significant a height gain you have achieved (for this altitude).

To reach the pilgrims' rest houses and tents near Driraphuk, which takes up to 2hrs from Damding Donkhang, remain on the right bank of the river and head to the semi-grassy area with the low buildings. Those staying at the monastery need to cross the river on a quaint log bridge. The walk, often across soft

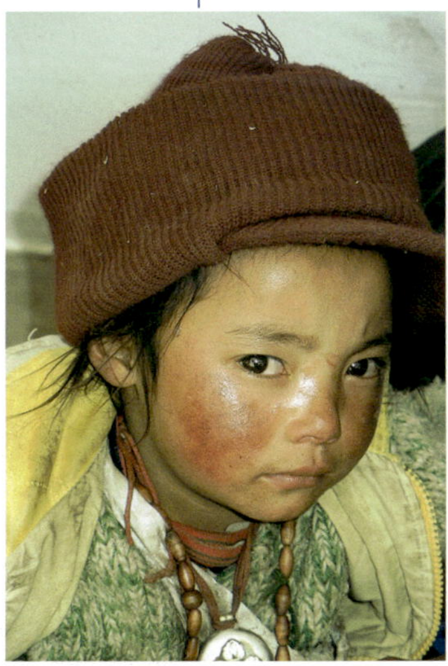

Nomad child at Damding Donkhang

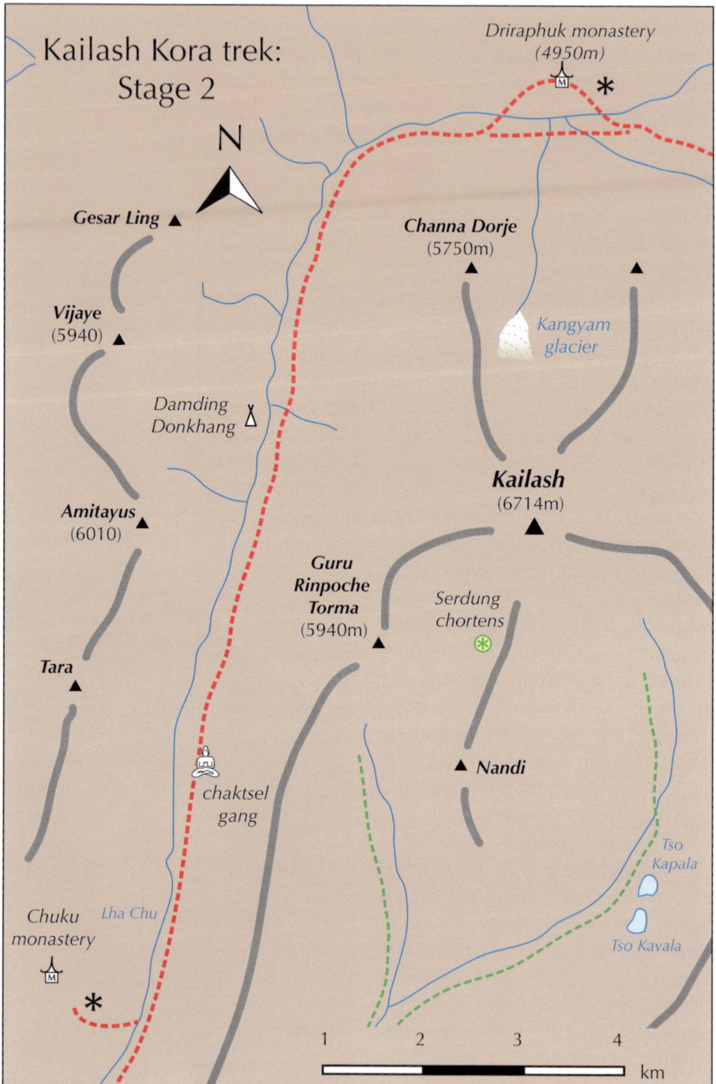
Kailash Kora trek:
Stage 2
N
Driraphuk monastery
(4950m)
Gesar Ling
Channa Dorje
(5750m)
Vijaye
(5940)
Kangyam
glacier
Damding
Donkhang
Kailash
(6714m)
Amitayus
(6010)
Guru
Rinpoche
Torma
(5940m)
Serdung
chortens
Tara
Nandi
chaktsel
gang
Tso
Kapala
Chuku
monastery
Lha Chu
Tso Kavala
1
2
3
4
km

Profile 2: Chuku monastery to Driraphuk monastery

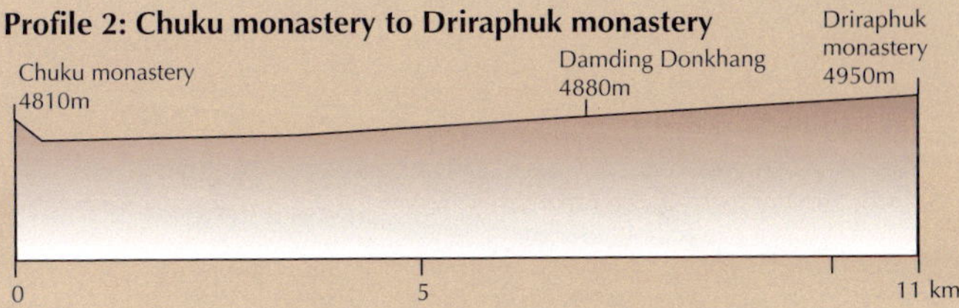

inviting meadows, is inspirational. The actions of time on once mighty peaks can be observed in these crumbling hillsides. Only Kailash resists such decay, bold and sublime, little disturbed by the geological attacks of passing millennia. It takes about 4hrs to walk from Chuku monastery to Driraphuk monastery along the east bank.

From the monastery the stunning north face of Kailash appears like a gigantic icy ogre guarded by craggy black sentinels. These guardian peaks are **Channa Dorje** (Vajrapani) on the west, **Jampelyang** (Manjushri) and **Chenresig** (Avalokiteshvara) on the east. Rising around 2000m, the north face of Kailash is reminiscent of the north wall of the Eiger from Grindelwald, but this face is not to be desecrated by the ungodly feet of man.

The monastery of Driraphuk (4950m) belongs to the Kagyu-pa order and was rebuilt in 1985. The name Driraphuk literally means 'cave of the female yak horns'. (Dri means female yak.) The monastery is built around a

THE NORTH FACE OF SHIVA'S THRONE

The forbidding hanging ice and snow of the north face is paralysed by the arctic temperatures and frozen in time. Here, icy avalanches and petrified white spider patterns cling forever on the horizontal layers. The throne of Shiva is sublime, a heavenly sight, at once an image of joy and of destructive horrors. No ordinary mortal would presume to tread here and invade the holiest cradle of the gods.

Kailash north face

small cave, which was used by the sage Gotsangpo around 1213 to 1217 for meditations. As for the female yak horns, legends relate that Gotsangpo was led to this shelter by a *dakini*, a protective female flying deity in the shape of a yak. The *dakini* or *khandroma*, also known as Senge Dongba, is a lion-faced deity. She also guards the inner pass of the Gangpo Sanglam La west of the Drolma La pass. The monastery has images of Chenresig (Avalokiteshvara) with Sakyamuni Buddha and Channa Dorje. The cave, which contains an image of Gotsangpo, is upstairs at the back of the main prayer hall.

Accommodation

The monastery guesthouse costs 45 Yuan per person in a four-bedded room. There are six beds in another room. More rooms below the *gompa* are under construction. Across the valley to the north are further rest houses used by pilgrims and visitors in the main season. Camping is also possible here.

Driraphuk, Cave of the Female Yak Horns

Eating out

No food was available here in 2005, but thermoses of boiled water were provided for a fee.

Some groups and individual parties choose to stay here a day for further acclimatisation and to visit the Kangyam glacier. The source of the Indus river is a three-day trek up the valley from Driraphuk for those with a special interest or much more time.

Day hike to Kangyam Glacier

Altitude range	4950m to 5400m
Time	3hrs
Distance	7km round trip
Altitude gain	450m
Altitude loss	450m
Highest point	5400m

To hike to the glacier, begin by heading down to cross the river at the bridge a little to the east of the monastery. The route then climbs steadily up, passing the pilgrims' rest houses and tents, and heads towards the obvious gap between the two guardian peaks. Soon the faint path deteriorates and becomes quite a scramble, so **take care** on icy sections. An accident around here is not to be contemplated! The striking glacier sits directly below the north face. Allow 2hrs or more to get there, depending on acclimatisation, and 1hr to return. ◂ From a Buddhist point of view this walk is only considered to be auspicious by devout pilgrims who have already completed 12 circuits of the Kora. Unless you have done so, you may not wish to incur any negative vibrations by attempting it.

Be extra vigilant on the return trip, as the path can be icy heading down.

STAGE 3:
Driraphuk to Shabje Draktok, via Drolma La

Altitude range	4950m to 5250m
Time	6–7hrs
Distance	10km
Altitude gain	710m
Altitude loss	410m
Highest point	5660m

The initial part of the trek to the Drolma La winds along a broad shelf to the north of the Drolma Chu river. From the monastery, head down across the river and then divert eastwards and steeply up. Those coming from the pilgrims' encampment follow a different path, also steeply up, and the two paths meet near the top of the shoulder of this first hill. Where the path levels out, about 1hr from the start, there is a grassy area known as **Jarok Donkhang**. The height here is approximately 5200m, and it is sometimes used as a camping spot for

Kailash north and east faces

groups. The Polung valley lies to the south. There is a glacier at the head of the valley, which can be reached in two to three hours from Jarok Donkhang.

To the southeast is the **Gangpo Sanglam La** pass (5675m), which offers an alternative, slightly shorter route into the eastern Lham Chu valley. The pass on this route is higher than the Drolma La and the trail is said to be hard underfoot and dangerous. Also this route is strictly for those pilgrims who have completed 12 Koras. It is said to be guarded by the spirit Khandroma, who might adopt a wrathful countenance if you invade her territory!

Your route now climbs steadily but not too steeply for about another 100m. There are amazing views of the north face of Kailash, and the edge of the mysterious, seldom seen east face rising above the shadowy, forbidding Polung valley, where useful medicinal herbs are reputed to grow. The river below your path is still the Drolma Chu. The climb is steady, but the effects of altitude make it very tiring. ▶

With a plethora of rugged towers and peaks in all directions, there are plenty of excuses to stop for rests and to take photographs.

The Shiva or **Shiwal Tsal** (5330m), also known to Indian pilgrims as the Vajra Yogini burial grounds, is an extraordinary place, looking like a rather untidy rubbish tip for worn-out clothes. To Tibetan Buddhist and Hindu pilgrims, this is the place of death. This is where Yamantaka (Dorje Jigje in Tibetan), the god of the dead, decides a person's fate at the gates of death. Pilgrims may be seen cutting off strips of clothing or depositing some of their hair. Some even lie down, feigning death. You may feel like trying this yourself for a rest! The symbolic acts performed by the pilgrims here are rituals that mark the death of their past life. They await a rebirth free from past sins on the pass ahead. It takes about 2hrs to reach this place from Driraphuk. Also venerated by Hindus is a small peak called Vajra Yogini, just to the left of the trail above the cremation grounds, where dead pilgrims and *lamas* are buried.

After the Shiva Tsal, the path climbs a bit and then again levels out. Take care around here, as makeshift altars and stone piles litter the path. A number of significant rocks are found along the next section before the final climb to the Drolma La pass. The Bardo Trang is a large rock with a narrow hollow beneath it. This gap is a measure of a pilgrim's level of sin. Anyone becoming stuck under this rock is deep in sin. Could any foreign trekker pass under it?

An altar of three rocks further on represents the Drubtak *shabje*, a spot where one can see a footprint of Milarepa. One of the magical contests between Milarepa and Naro Bonchung took place here. The Dhikpa Kar Nak rock encountered shortly afterwards is another sin-testing spot. Again, devout pilgrims will attempt to

Profile 3: Driraphuk monastery to Shabje Draktok

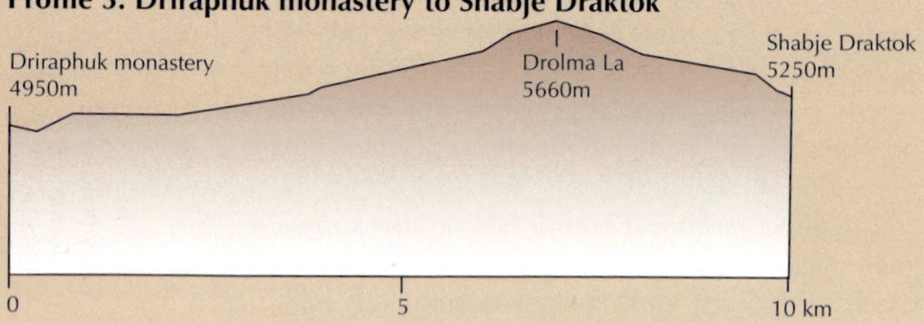

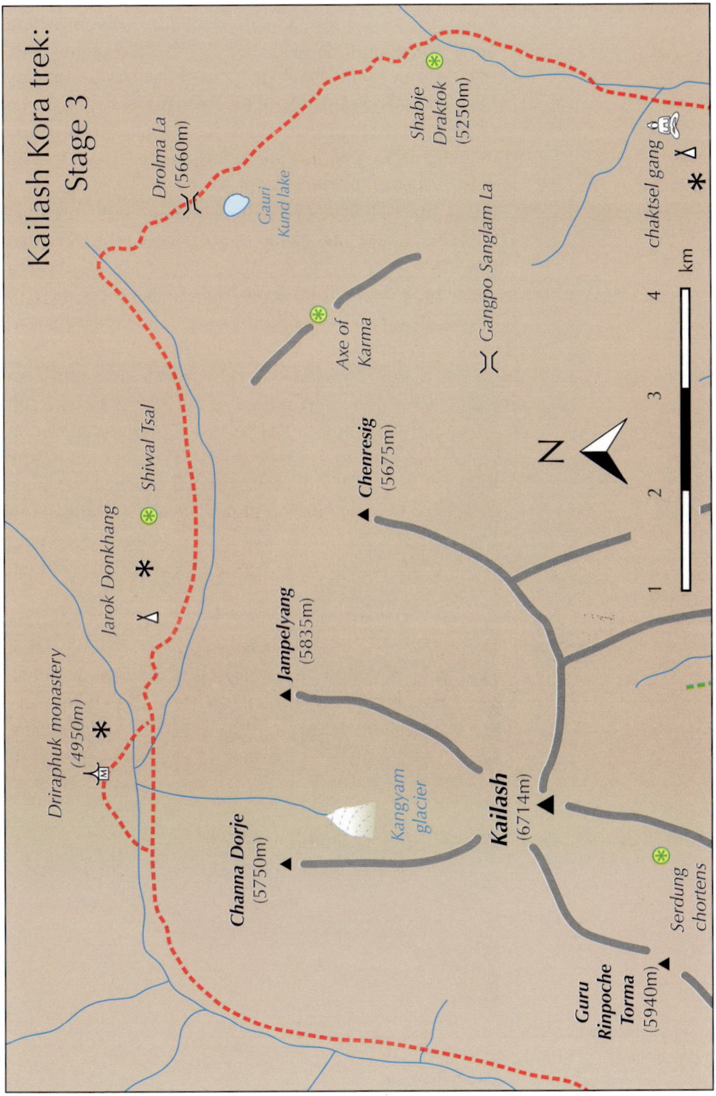
Kailash Kora trek: Stage 3
Drolma La (5660m)
Gauri Kund lake
Shabje Draktok (5250m)
chaktsel gang
Axe of Karma
Gangpo Sanglam La
Shiwal Tsal
Jarok Donkhang
Driraphuk monastery (4950m)
Jampelyang (5835m)
Chenresig (5675m)
N
1
2
3
4
km
Kangyam glacier
Kailash (6714m)
Channa Dorje (5750m)
Serdung chortens
Guru Rinpoche Torma (5940m)

squeeze through the tunnels here. This act symbolises entry to hell and elevation beyond. The forbidding peak to the south here is Sharma Ri, which pilgrims consider to be a vision of hell. It casts an eerie shadow on the pass later in the day.

The trail continues on, climbing gently to a stream (often frozen) at the foot of the Drolma La pass. It is about 3hrs trek to this point. The stream is called Shenpe Diklak Chu and has significance for butchers, who suffer from ill karma due to their work. Pilgrims often rest a while here, taking sustenance before the final push for rebirth ahead on the pass.

Tibetan pilgrims rest before the Drolma La pass climb

COLOURFUL TIBETAN PILGRIMS

A group of colourful Tibetan pilgrims rest at Shenpe Diklak Chu. According to their dress style (the women have red and green tongue-like sashes stitched into the fabric on the back of their coats), they are from northwestern Tibet, from a region close to Rutok.

The final ascent from here to the pass is steep, unrelenting and energy-sapping. If ever there was a spot for an overdose of glucose tablets, this is it. The path traverses rocky terrain with some large boulders, most of which have religious significance. One of the more important ones, called Mila Shugtri, has the mantra of 'Om Mani Padme Hum' ('Hail to the lotus flower') carved on it. Butter is smeared here and pilgrims touch it with their heads. Gyalpo Norling Phoprang, which means 'residence of Kubera, the King of Wealth', is the Tibetan name for the icy peaks visible before the Drolma La. ▸

After about 40mins up this last ascent, the pass can be seen across a less severe slope. At this altitude, you can expect quite deep snow. The Drolma (Dolma) La pass itself can then be reached more easily in less than

The trail can be exceedingly slippery with icy snow up here, so it is important to overcome any disorientation or balance problems from altitude sickness before tackling these obstacles.

A WAKE-UP CALL?

Before you are the colourful prayer flags and the mystical Drolma La, beckoning you on. Into thin air at 5660m, the view is literally breathtaking. At last you are on top of the world, in a land of dreams (or nightmares). What joy fills the weary soul, perhaps the first real sense of spiritual rebirth. The release of tension having reached the pass is palpable. Perhaps this is what they mean by a spiritual wake-up call? After all this, are you really free of past sins?

Gauri Kund lake below the Drolma La pass (south side)

15–20mins, about an hour from the base of the pass. Innumerable prayer flags festoon the summit and these almost completely obscure the actual Drolma stone boulder itself. Wind is often the greatest problem on this pass, but the air can sometimes be still, sparkling and crystal clear.

The Drolma La pass is the pass of the deity Tara. It stands at the dizzy height of 5660m and marks the summit of the 'hill of salvation'. It offers every pilgrim a window to spiritual renewal, a transition from their old life to a new one, cleansed of all previous sins. Passing pilgrims leave prayer flags and tourists are also advised to leave flags at the pass. Everyone needs a little luck right here, as the descent can be icy and sometimes treacherous in deep snow.

Before leaving the pass, take a look at the large Drolma stone. Tibetans call it Phawang Mebar and perform a number of auspicious rituals here. According to legend, another large stone behind it marks the spot where 21 wolves melted into the rock. These mythical wolves relate to the 21 incarnationas of Tara. Earlier the same wolves had led the sage and explorer of Kailash, Gotsangpo, to this pass rather than the Gangpo Sanglam pass of the dakini.

The descent is immediate and rocky underfoot, in this landscape of shattered and decaying cliffs and peaks. A 400m descent of difficult and at times treacherous trail lies ahead, so relish the views here before you start. Below the pass and in view is the Tukje Chenpo Tso or, to Hindus, **Gauri Kund** lake (5440m). This is the lake of compassion, which is a deep turquoise colour when not frozen.

Some hardy Hindus like to take a ritual bath in the lake if it is unfrozen. It is said that he who bathes here will remove all diseases; they are more likely to get severe hypothermia! Another legend says that Shiva's consort, Parvati, meditated here to win over Shiva as her lover. The lake is reputedly very deep; some say more than 25m, and its deep turquoise colour certainly suggests so. Sometimes the ice of the lake appears to be grumbling, as if lurking demons are trapped within.

LEGEND OF GAURI KUND LAKE (TUKJE CHENPO TSO)

The God of Wealth, Jambhala (Kubera), and his family often used the lake for washing themselves. One day a woman pilgrim came to wash, but her baby fell off her back into the lake and was drowned. So the guardian deity decided to freeze the lake to stop such a thing happening again.

derived from *Three Years in Tibet* by Ekai Kawaguchi

The route now heads down around the top of the lake to a small crest adorned by rock cairns and prayer flags. The view from here unfolds and the path can be seen, often deep in snow. Ahead are the distant valley walls and peaks above the Lham Chu valley with **Sonam Ri** floating above it. The valley of the Lham Chu drains the country northeast of the Kora route and is used by nomads to access grazing pasture well to the north of the Kangtise range via the Nangwa La pass.

Some care is needed on this long slope in icy conditions.

◂ There are further crags of shattered rock and then, to the west, is an astonishing rock formation on the skyline. This strange, angry-looking formation is known as the **Axe of Karma**, emblem of the King of Death. But it is powerless under the spell of Drolma (Tara). Nature's

Nomad tent at Shabje Draktok

power here is much in evidence; the cliffs and rock walls are breaking apart and shattering under the frosty spell of arctic temperatures.

It may take up to 1hr to slip and slide down in bad conditions to the lip of the valley. The trail here often divides, taking differing routes to avoid the worst of the ice; the conditions underfoot vary considerably. ▸

The last descent, to the floor and the valley of the eastern Buddha 'Akshobhya', is quite steep, with loose rocks underfoot.

The general lethargy you may have felt when crossing the Drolma La will dissipate here. The sight of a nomad encampment below, with the promise of hot tea, is enough to revive anyone's flagging spirit. From the pass to this refreshment stop can easily take 2hrs. This is called **Shabje Draktok** (5250m), after another Buddha footprint nearby.

STAGE 4: *Shabje Draktok to Zutrulphuk monastery*

Altitude range	5250m to 4835m
Time	3–4hrs
Distance	11km
Altitude loss	400m
Highest point	5250m

From Shabje Draktok the wide gentle valley of the Lham Chu sweeps down under less severe peaks and ridges. It provides for relaxing, pleasant walking with some green grassy spots and silver streams of clear water. Initially the main path is on the east bank of the river and well defined. About 30mins down the valley, you should cross the river, which at this point is fairly easily forded on stones and rocks. Leaving this crossing too late may severely reduce the temperature of your feet, as the river becomes deeper and there are no proper bridging points. There is a footprint of Milarepa between Shabje Draktok and the valley of the *dakini*, the **Gangpo Sanglam Chu**. A

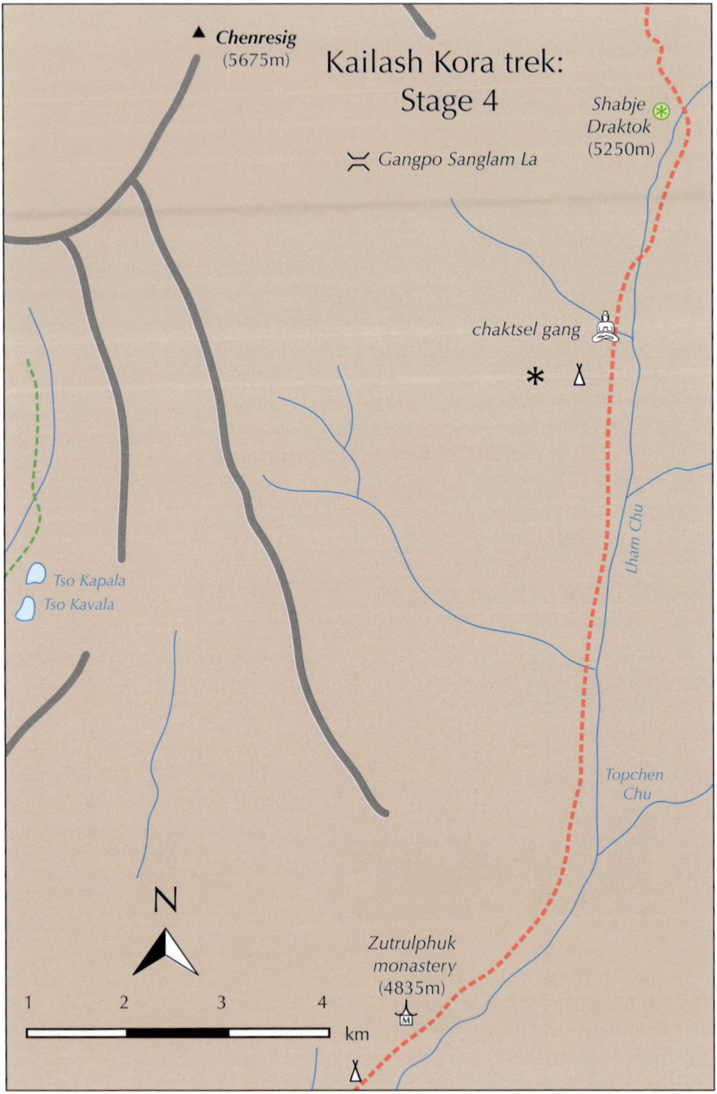
Chenresig
(5675m)
Kailash Kora trek:
Stage 4
Shabje
Draktok
(5250m)
Gangpo Sanglam La
chaktsel gang
Lham Chu
Tso Kapala
Tso Kavala
Topchen
Chu
N
Zutrulphuk
monastery
(4835m)
1
2
3
4
km

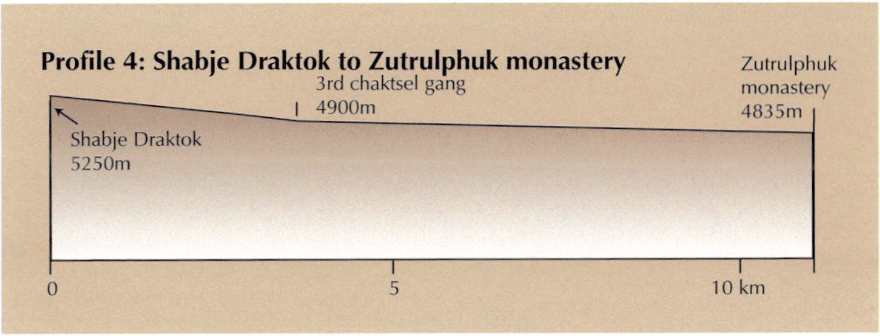

third *chaktsel gang* prostration point for pilgrims is located at the entrance to this tributary from the west. Here the often-obscured eastern crystal face of Kailash deigns to show its face again. Trekking parties may well camp close to the third *chaktsel gang* point in order to catch the view at sunrise. The time from Driraphuk to here is about 7hrs.

The eastern valley of the Kora is often known as the valley of Milarepa, the poet, ascetic and hermit. He is, according to storytellers, the defender of Kailash for the Buddhist faithful. One of his legendary fights with the Bon deity Naro Bonchung took place near here. It takes

Kailash east face

Zutrulphuk monastery

about 2hrs from Shabje Draktok to reach the junction of the **Lham Chu** and the **Topchen Chu**, which joins the main valley from the east. The Lham Chu, which later becomes called the **Zhong Chu**, turns to the southwest around here and after a further hour's walking, below dark crags on the right of the path, the path reaches **Zutrulphuk monastery**. Allow at least 9hrs for the total walk between Driraphuk and Zutrulphuk monasteries.

The rebuilt monastery of Zutrulphuk sits on the site of the miracle cave of Milarepa. A statue of the saint in normal pose with his listening ear can be seen in the monastery chapel. The cave is where both Milarepa and Naro Bonchung sheltered when rain fell, and was another place where the contest to gain control of Kailash was fought out. The final magical duel concluded on the summit of Kailash, with Naro Bonchung falling off the top. As he fell, his drum is said to have gorged out the step-like features on the south face. The vanquished Bonpo was given a mountain near Lake Manasarovar on which to reside. This peak, east of Kailash, is called **Bon Ri** (not to be confused with another mountain in Eastern Tibet also sacred to Bonpo).

Accommodation

The monastery has three rooms attached to its courtyard. One has three beds; the other two have floor space. Cost 45 Yuan each bed; dormitory floor 25 Yuan. More accommodation is available below the monastery during the season.

STAGE 5
Zutrulphuk to Darchen

Altitude range	4835m to 4650m
Time	3–4hrs
Distance	12km
Altitude gain	15m
Altitude loss	200m
Highest point	4850m

From the monastery the path heads down gently on the right bank of the river, most likely in shade first thing in the morning, so keep well clothed. There are a few very small rises as the path winds its way down. After about 1hr you will enter what is known as the **Trangmar Gorge**, not initially much of a gorge. ▸

The route climbs along this deepening canyon with vivid rocks and slopes. The colours range from yellow and orange to green, red, purple and black.

Trangmar gorge

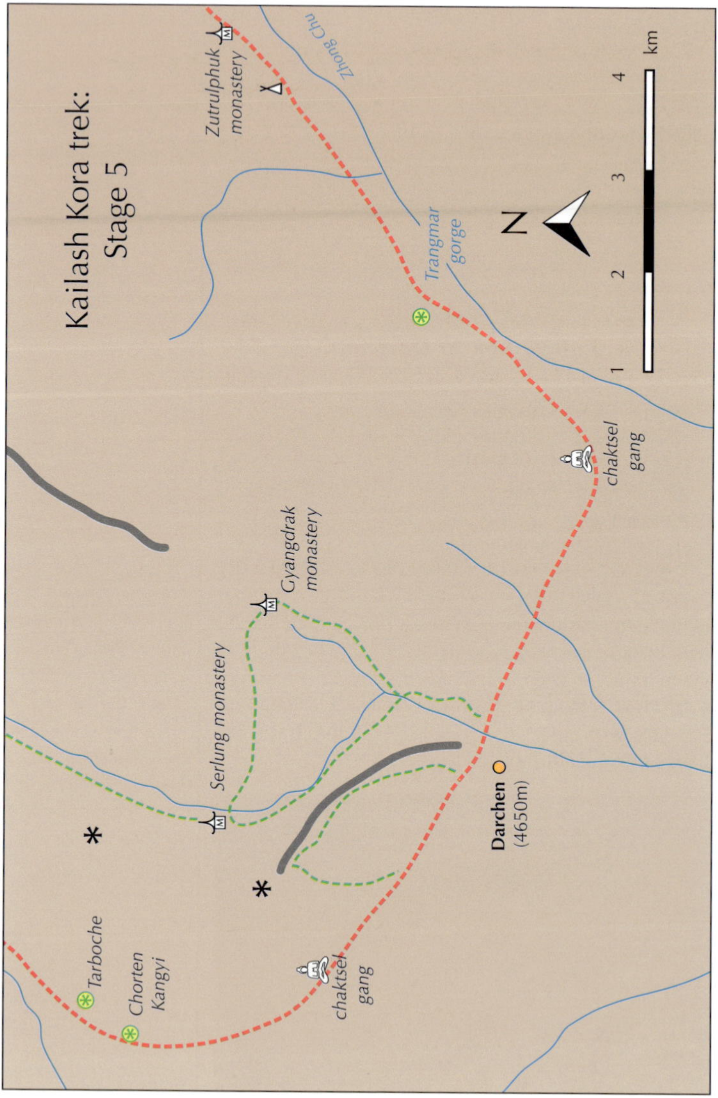
Kailash Kora trek:
Stage 5
Zutrulphuk monastery
Zhong Chu
Trangmar gorge
N
1
2
3
4
km
chaktsel gang
Gyangdrak monastery
Serlung monastery
Darchen
(4650m)
Tarboche
Chorten Kangyi
chaktsel gang

Profile 5: Zutrulphuk monastery to Darchen

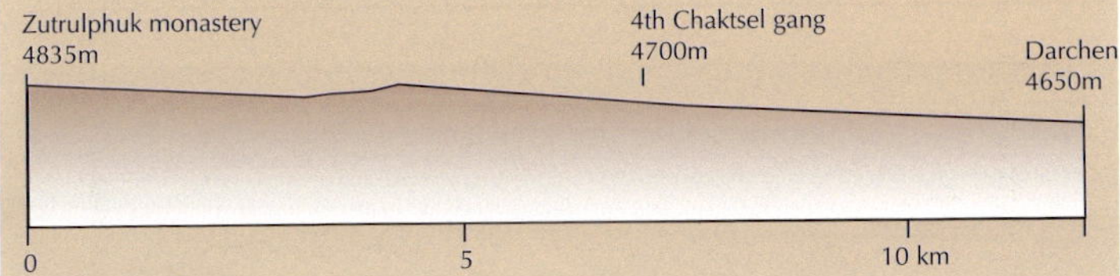

You need to **take particular care** at one point where the path slopes off slightly towards the deep gorge below.

The trail makes one more attempt to drain the weary pilgrim here, as it climbs to a rocky knoll. Then all sense of exhaustion evaporates, as your climb reveals the morning splendour of Gurla Mandhata and the Nepal Himalayas to the south. A very short descent brings you to the last prostration point or *chaktsel gang*. Also near here is a checkpost and a couple of teashops. The last amble of the Kora takes an hour or more, crossing a dry river bed (which may have water in it during monsoon or periods of snow melt) and passing some *mani* walls. In Darchen, a final river is crossed and the Kora walk is complete.

Remember, although your previous sins may have been forgiven, you must do 13 circuits of the mountain to be forever cleansed!

OTHER TREKS IN THE KAILASH REGION

Trekking the Kora, upper Lha Chu valley

1 Darchen Day Walks

Darchen ridge walk

Altitude range	4650m to 5200m
Time	6–7 hrs
Distance	8km round trip
Altitude gain	550m
Highest point	5200m

This is a fabulous walk by any standards. It will give unparalleled views of the Himalayas, as well as the southern, sapphire face of Kailash and the Inner Kora area. The timings quoted here assume that you have already acclimatised after completing the Kora. Don't expect to be following any obvious trails, as there are none on this ridge walk. At well over 5000m, it is a fair weather walk and should be treated as such. Be prepared for wind or sudden weather changes; take food and plenty of water. An accident around here is to be avoided at all costs.

The trail (such as it is) begins behind the *chorten* and long *mani* wall at the top of Darchen village. Study the cliff carefully from below before beginning your ascent, as once you are on the cliff it is hard to see the rest of the trail. The start is little more than a lung-busting scramble up behind the east end of the *mani* wall, but don't be deterred by this rough beginning. There are two paths, which soon converge and become ill defined in the rocky scree-like slope below the main cliff faces. After some more scrambling to the west, you should find an obvious gap in the rock face. It might be necessary to hold on to both sides of this defile to aid the scramble up.

Once through this narrow gap, the going is easier. A path zigzags up to the lower prayer flags. The more prolific prayer flags of the main shrine are further up the

Gyangdrak monastery

ridge, about 45mins from the start. In order to continue along the ridge, it is easier to go around to the right side of the flags although, spiritually-speaking, this is the wrong way unless you are a Bon pilgrim. Heading up behind the flags, you reach a *mani* wall about 1hr from Darchen. Again it is easier to follow a faint trail up on the right of the wall, rather than walking on the left (the correct) side.

From the end of the wall, head northwest for 30mins up the trail to the next crest. This is the point where many pilgrims will do prostrations, because there is a stunning view of Kailash here. Ahead the landscape is less steep and now you need to head initially in the direction of Kailash on an indistinct trail towards some stone *chortens*. It is easier to head left of these and climb steadily. The monastery of Gyangdrak is visible across the valley to the north.

Ahead is a tempting-looking summit adorned with prayer flags. Do not head up to this highpoint but skirt around its base, clockwise, heading west. There are some indistinct tracks and stone markers around its base area. The hypnotic view of Kailash is lost now, but turn

Kailash from the ridge above Darchen

around for an equally mesmerising sight. To the south sparkle the tremendous peaks of the northwestern Nepalese Dolpo region, Gurla Mandhata, Api, Saipal, Nampur and peaks of the Indian Garhwal.

Having skirted the tempting peak, head up the crest to the north, as best suits your breathing. From here there is a great view of the Inner Kora area of Kailash. Just to the west, left up the ridge, are some small rock outcrops, which offer shelter should there be any wind. This place makes a great photo stop and Serlung monastery is also visible below. It takes around 2hrs to reach this glorious spot from Darchen.

From here walk on down the ridge for about 10 mins to a wide, broad col. In order to reach the highest point of the ridge ahead, climb up the next hill and aim for a lower saddle between the two summits in front of you on the ridge. This might be best achieved by keeping to the north side of the two summits. The last summit, which is the highest point of the ridge walk, can be reached from the saddle between those two summits. This high point, at about 5200m, gives an amazing, unobstructed view all around. Down to the west is a view of the Kora and

Indian Himalayas from Tibet

the Chorten Kangyi. To the north and east is the outlier, Nandi, and Kailash itself. To the south, floating above Lakes Manasarovar and Rakhas Tal, is the whole Himalayan chain, stretching from central Nepal to Kamet and Ladakh in the far west. To the east, you can make out Bonri. To reach this heavenly view might take 3 to 4hrs, depending on photo stops and your level of acclimatisation.

To return to Darchen, the simplest option is to retrace your steps. However, to vary the descent, it is possible to return a different way; just watch out for impenetrable gullies that may block your way. Head back down to the wide, broad col and then down the slope towards Darchen. The road and Kora track can be seen far below. In general, try to head over to the left at this point. You can aim for a point on the lower crest where you see the road into Darchen hit the ridge line below. This spot is in a similar direction to Gurla Mandhata. Cross a small gully, but don't go too far east, as there are deeper gullies which will stop you in your tracks. This area is about 20mins from the viewpoint.

If you get to a deep ravine you are too far to the east, so head back and, once clear of gullies, head straight downhill. About 35mins from the viewpoint you should be able to aim down between the now more obvious gullies that are too deep to cross. Lower down you may need to tend over to your right, to the west, to avoid more gullies. Near the bottom you need to head generally southwest to see a cairn on the edge of the big ravine on your right. Zigzag down from here to the Kora trail. You should be just a little east of the settlement houses below. The whole descent takes about 1hr. Once on the Kora trail, become a Bonpo and head east. In around 15mins there is a prayer wheel *mani* wall and another 15mins brings you back to Darchen.

Gyangdrak monastery

Altitude range	4650m to 4970m
Time	4–5hrs
Distance	8km round trip
Altitude gain	320m
Highest point	4970m

A new dirt track wide enough for 4x4 vehicles now climbs out of Darchen and heads for **Gyangdrak monastery**. The initial zigzag climb is quite steep for hiking. Following this track for around 2–3 hrs takes you to the monastery, which sits dramatically on a high perch. The monastery has now been rebuilt and is a centre for the Drigung Kagyu-pa sect, whose monks helped to restore it.

Serlung monastery

Altitude range	4650m to 4750m
Time	3–4hrs
Distance	10km round trip
Altitude gain	100m
Highest point	4750m

Serlung valley below Kailash

To walk to **Serlung monastery**, follow the wide track from Darchen that goes to **Gyangdrak**. After about 1hr, turn left at the junction and head up the valley westwards. It takes about 2hrs to reach this monastery from Darchen. It has now been partially restored and the main chapel is complete.

It is possible to visit both monasteries on a longer 7–8hr walk. In keeping with Buddhist traditions, you should do this in a clockwise direction – heading first to Serlung and then over the pass between the two valleys to Gyangdrak – but this makes a harder walk. The easier option is to go to Gyangdrak first. From the crest of the main pass, some very fit climbers or trekkers and sherpas have climbed and scrambled up the ridge to the north for an amazing view over Nandi and the Inner Kora area, but this is not recommended for non-climbers.

2 Inner Kora

Altitude range	4650m to 5900m
Time	3–5 days
Distance	approx 25km
Altitude gain	1250m
Highest point	5900m

The Inner Kora is also called the Nandi Parikrama by Hindus and takes 3–5 days to complete. This is a pilgrimage that should be undertaken only by those Buddhists who have completed 13 normal Koras. Non-Hindu and non-Buddhist visitors should note that **this is a walk for seasoned mountaineers only** and involves some dangerously steep sections. We have not attempted this route. The following information comes from various Hindu writers.

Heading up the **Serlung Chu** river valley from Serlung monastery, there are a number of caves in the

Kailash south face

The route of the Inner Kora is difficult and dangerous, particularly below the treacherous great gully.

mountain to the west sometimes referred to as Asthapad (not Kailash, which Jains call Asthapada). The amazing 'rock chest' of Nandi is known as Neten Yenlakzung by Tibetans. ◂ Here snow, ice and rocks tumble constantly to form a great ice mound, below which the ill-defined route winds around moraines. After this, a very steep ascent starts to the pass.

Right under the colossal south face of Kailash there used to stand 19 *chortens*, known as the **Serdung Chuksum chortens**. These chortens belong to the Drigung Kagyu-pa sect. Traditionally there should have been just 13: *ser* means gold, *dung* means *stupa/chorten* and *chuksum* means 13. There are now only 13 and they have been restored. They are set back into a long horizontal crack-like overhang, which offers some protection from crashing snow. Four *chortens* on the west are separated by a cluster of prayer flags from nine more on the east. The wall at the back of the ledge is painted the traditional red colour.

The Inner Kora then climbs between **Nandi** and **Kailash**, a climb which is said to be fraught with avalanching snow and stonefall. The climb is in the order of 500m. The Saptarishi cave, set high in the face of Kailash near the Nandi 'pass' on the Nandi Kora, is located at about 5900m. From the top there is an equally steep descent. On this side of the Inner Kora are two small lakes. The **Tso Kapala**, often known as *rukta*, the black lake, is around 150m across and retains its dark colour due to the black rocks on its bed. The other lake, which is twice the size, is called the **Tso Kavala**. This lake, in contrast, is white – the *durchi* or milky lake. This lake is said to hold the keys to Kailash.

3 LAKE MANASAROVAR

Lake Manasarovar is called Mapham Tso in Tibetan and lies below the impressive hulk of Gurla Mandhata. South of the lake, the Himalayas stretch east and west in a never-ending ribbon of wonder. The lake has many moods and is famous for its changing colours, its infinite variations of light and its fearsome storms.

While Kailash is considered to be the male aspect, Lake Manasarovar is regarded as the complementary female aspect of this holy region. Hindus believe the lake was created from the mind of the God of Creation, Brahma. The lake is mentioned in ancient Hindu scriptures dating from at least 500 years before Christ. Its name is recorded in the famous epic of India, the Ramayana. For a Hindu, drinking even a single drop of its holy purifying waters is believed to cleanse the sins of a hundred lives. The meaning of Manas is 'light' or 'sun', and the lake has an amazing turquoise colour under clear skies.

A LEGEND OF MANASAROVAR

From the top of Kailash, Shiva and Parvati sat in prayer for 12 long years. During all that time no rain fell, so they called on Brahma because they could not wash. Brahma created the lake for them. Feeling cleaner now, they continued to offer devotion to Kailash and a golden *lingam* then appeared in the lake.

Buddhists believe that Maya, the mother of the earthly Buddha, Gautama Siddhartha, washed in Lake Manasarovar prior to the birth of her son. Tibetans believe the lake was born through devotional acts such as giving, personal generosity and from those genuinely seeking enlightenment.

LAKE MANASAROVAR CIRCUIT TREK

Lake Manasarovar is approximately 90–100km in circumference. Before the Cultural Revolution, there were eight monasteries around the lake.

The Lake Manasarovar *parikrama* – or walk around the lake – can be can be done in four days, but five allows for a more relaxed pace. Most pilgrims begin from the village at Chui monastery on the west side, while others begin from the village of Hor, on the north-east side. Aside from Hor, Chui and the odd monastery dormitory, there few places to stay, so expect to do some camping. This is essentially a fully self-supporting trek. The following is only a brief outline of the route. The walking stages indicated do not necessarily coincide with daily stages. The altitude hovers around and a little above 4550m.

STAGE 1:
Chui monastery to Hor

Time	8–9hrs
Distance	24km

The section north and east from **Chui monastery** climbs above the cliff. There are a number of meditation caves in the cliffs, accessed from the lakeshore. The route passes the **ruins of Cherkip monastery** and comes to **Langpona monastery**. The northern end of the lake is

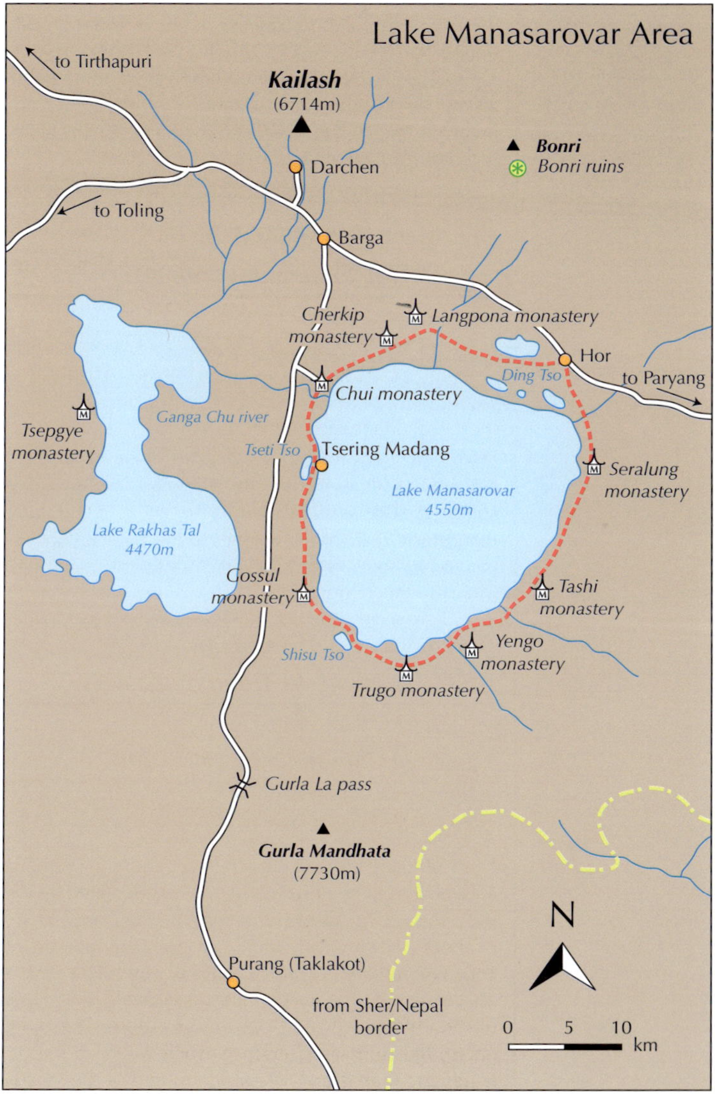
Lake Manasarovar Area
to Tirthapuri
Kailash
(6714m)
Darchen
Bonri
Bonri ruins
to Toling
Barga
Cherkip monastery
Langpona monastery
Hor
Ding Tso
to Paryang
Chui monastery
Ganga Chu river
Tsepgye monastery
Tseti Tso
Tsering Madang
Seralung monastery
Lake Manasarovar
4550m
Lake Rakhas Tal
4470m
Gossul monastery
Tashi monastery
Yengo monastery
Shisu Tso
Trugo monastery
Gurla La pass
Gurla Mandhata
(7730m)
N
Purang (Taklakot)
from Sher/Nepal border
0 5 10
km

Unless you are visiting in the depths of winter, when the lake is frozen, it may well be necessary to skirt around further to the north to reach Hor.

marshy, with several smaller lakes. ◂ Basic guesthouses and a couple of local cafés exist in the expanding village of **Hor**. The route marked on some maps along the shoreline is impractical, as the difficulties involved in crossing rivers and avoiding marshy areas here are substantial.

STAGE 2:
Hor to Seralung monastery

Time	3–4hrs
Distance	13km

From Hor you must rejoin the trail close to the lake beyond the shores of the small **Ding Tso** lake. Heading south, it takes around 3–4hrs to walk to **Seralung monastery**. This *gompa* belongs to the Drigung Kagyu-pa, and has been reconstructed close to its original site.

STAGE 3:
Seralung to Trugo monastery

Time	7hrs
Distance	25km

From **Seralung** the trail crosses flatter country. The ruins and remains of two monasteries are encountered on the walk, these being **Tashi** and **Yengo**. The **Tag Tsangpo** river is about halfway from Seralung. From the remains of **Yengo monastery** to **Trugo monastery** may take a further 4hrs. According to tradition, the Indian master Atisha meditated here, although the place is now a Gelug-pa establishment. There is a guesthouse at Trugo.

Gurla Mandhata and Lake Manasarovar

STAGE 4:
Trugo monastery to Gossul monastery

Time	4–5hrs
Distance	16km

The trail follows the lakeshore, with some swampy sections and some firm ground depending on the season. Continuing on around the southwest corner of the lake, you come to the smaller lake of **Shisu Tso**. Memo Nani, better known as Gurla Mandhata (7730m), dominates the southern shores of the lake. Gossul monastery has good views over the sometimes tempestuous lake.

There is one basic guesthouse here.

STAGE 5:
Gossul monastery to Chui monastery

Time	6hrs
Distance	20km

From Gossul monastery, the trail keeps fairly close to the lake all the way to Chui monastery, passing Tsering Madang and the tiny Tseti Tso lake. A large resthouse used by Hindu visitors is located close to the shore, below the monastery and the main village of Chui, and there is an acceptable guesthouse in Chui village.

CHUI VILLAGE RIDGE WALK

Altitude range	4600m to 4780m
Time	1hr
Distance	2km round trip
Altitude gain	180m
Altitude loss	180m
Highest point	4780m

This short 1hr trek is a great walk for acclimatisation at high altitude. Leave Chui village to the south and head up the low ridge to a *chorten* decorated with yak horns. Already Kailash has appeared to the north and Chui monastery looks quite imposing across the ravine. Continue up along the ridge, but try to take some short zigzags nearer the top as it becomes steeper. After a false crest, slow down or the final lung-busting scramble will leaving you gasping for oxygen.

Once at the prayer flag-adorned summit, a magnificent panorama unfolds. Kailash, though distant, stands

Chui village, Ganga Chu river and Kailash

in dominant pose to the north, and to the south is the great mass of Gurla Mandhata. To the east Lake Manasarovar spreads out below the Nepalese Dolpo peaks, and to the west is the brooding lake Rakhas Tal. For some variety and an unobstructed view of the Indian Himalayan peaks to the southwest, take a more westerly descent from the summit back to Chui village.

4 LAKE RAKHAS TAL

Lake Rakhas Tal is the twin lake of the Kailash region, lying west of Lake Manasarovar. It has different names: in Hindu mythology it becomes the Ravena Soravar, the demon lake, while the Tibetan visitor will call it Langak Tso. It is 16m lower than Manasarovar, and there is a channel linking the two.

Geographically it is linked to the source of the Sutlej river through a trickle from the northwest side. The true source of the Sutlej river is not clear, because there are a number of significant rivers draining the northern slopes of the Indian Himalayas that join the river near its source area. Rakhas Tal also gets some water directly from Kailash. The lake is smaller than its dominant neighbour and has two islands of note within its confines: Lachato and Topserma. Tsepgye (also written Chepgey) monastery is the only one to be found on its shores.

Rakhas Tal suffers from a negative press from its pilgrim visitors. Its waters do not give any therapeutic aid and it is the habitat of evil creatures – the Rakshas, the demons of Hindu mythology who reside here –as well as unsuspecting flocks of Brahminy ducks.

The river that runs between the two lakes is called the Ganga Chu. It remained dry for about thirty years during the 'dark age' of Tibet's occupation. Today water runs here again, which is considered to be highly auspicious.

5 Tirthapuri

Tirthapuri is about 70km southwest of Darchen and about 10km south of Moincer (Mensi), close to the Sutlej river. This is the third holy pilgrimage site of the Kailash region. Its hot medicinal springs offer pilgrims a ritual wash and bathe. The size of the small monastery belies its greater significance as the place where Guru Rinpoche and his consort Yeshe Tsogyal meditated. Yeshe Tsogyal wrote down the teachings of Guru Rinpoche that have been and will again be resurrected in times of need. Tirthapuri is also the gateway to Khyunglung, the Garuda valley of the ancient Bon and Shangshung.

It is possible to follow a *kora* walk at Tirthapuri. The sights include cremation grounds, *mani* walls, piles of yak horns and a small hill pass. Close by are the famous multi-coloured strata of the cliffs, in white, yellow and brownish-red.

Accommodation

One guesthouse (primitive) 30–40 Yuan

Coloured cliffs near Khyunglung and Tirthapuri

THE GUGE KINGDOM

The following information outlines a trip to Tsaparang and Toling. From the point of view of improving altitude acclimatisation for the Kailash Kora, this three-day option is best done **before** the main *kora* trek. The region lies at an approximate altitude of 3800m.

Tsaparang citadel

Brief History and Cultural Aspects

The history of the Guge kingdom is the story of the Buddhist revival in Tibet as a whole. After the assassination of the pro-Bon King Langdarma, anarchy and lawlessness followed. However, Namde Wosung (O Sung), his pious son, settled in Toling and began the renaissance of Buddhism. Later Nyima Gon, the older of two grandsons of Langdarma, also resided in Guge and effectively became one of the most influential characters in Western Tibet.

When he died, his three sons inherited the three regions known as Maryul (Ladakh), Guge and Purang. The eldest son ruled Ladakh and established the Lhachen dynasty. The two younger sons ruled the regions of western Guge (Spiti) and eastern Guge (Purang).

The next pivotal character in the history of this area was Nyima Gon's grandson Kor De. He is more famously known as Lama Yeshe O and is thought to have lived between 947 and 1024AD. Yeshe O and his nephew Changchup O were the most pious of the Guge kings.

Yeshe O was instrumental in developing Toling and its monastic centre. The nearby fort and monastery of Tsaparang became the capital of the Guge region. At this time the region was virtually surrounded by the powerful Muslim sultans of Kashgar and Kashmir. This Muslim presence, while not a direct threat, hampered trade in Guge, but Buddhism flourished there through contacts with India. Ironically, in India, where it spread more rapidly, Buddhism was later almost completely eclipsed by the rise of Hinduism and virtually annihilated by the Muslim Mughals.

Wishing to enhance Buddhism in Tibet, Yeshe O instructed his followers to arrange for the great Indian master, Atisha, to be brought to Toling. Atisha, known as Jowo Je in Tibet, spent three years in Toling monastery around 1040AD. He reformed the Buddhist teachings of

Toling, Yeshe O temple chortens

the older Tantric Nyingma-pa and the Bon, creating the Kadam-pa doctrines. He also worked closely with Rinchen Zangpo, the famous translator or *lotsawa*.

RINCHEN ZANGPO

Rinchen Zangpo (958–1055AD) worked in Toling and throughout greater Guge. Sometimes referred to as the Lotsawa, which means translator, Rinchen Zangpo also took an interest in the Bon and, in particular, the ancient language of Shangshung. At the time of Rinchen Zangpo, the Guge kingdom extended across the Himalayas to the region of Kinnaur and Spiti in India. Its influence reached Zanskar and parts of Ladakh, now in India. Rinchen Zangpo is credited with establishing 108 monasteries. Toling and Tsaparang in Tibet, Nako, Lalung and Tabo in Kinnaur/Spiti, and Alchi in Ladakh, are the most well known sites that survive today, with their fabulous Kashmiri/Nepali inspired paintings.

The kingdom of Guge prospered until around 1100AD, when it lost some of its autonomy to the Ladakhi kings. It managed to avoid any serious threats from the Mongolians, partly because they too had adopted Buddhism as a state religion. The Guge kingdom remained a cohesive and relatively intact region for seven centuries. Many monasteries flourished in this peaceful but harsh and isolated region locked behind the Himalayas.

The next major event was the appearance of western visitors in 1624. Antonio de Andrade, a Portuguese Jesuit missionary, crossed the Indian Himalayas into Tibet over the Manas pass. At the time many pilgrims were dying on these high passes and for years it was assumed that they were killed by the 'noxious vapours' that were said to be found at these altitudes. We now know that this was altitude sickness. In August 1624 the missionaries arrived at Tsaparang. Surprisingly, perhaps, a strong bond was established between them and the Guge royal family.

At Easter 1626 the first church foundations were consecrated in Tibet at Tsaparang. The church was completed in August and, soon after, other missionaries arrived. Andrade himself left Tsaparang just before 1630 but some believe that the consequences of the mission in Tsaparang may have contributed to the downfall of Guge. The powerful King Sengge Namgyal of Ladakh feared the foreign religious intrusion and probably connived with the Tsaparang *lamas* to overthrow the Guge monarch. Other Tibetan historians, on the other hand, believe that the difficulties in Guge may have been arisen from a quarrel between Ladakh and Guge over a royal bride.

After a brief skirmish between Ladakh and Tibet, a treaty was signed in 1665 that eventually led to the partition of Guge. The Spiti and Kinnaur regions came under Ladakhi jurisdiction, while Toling remained with Tibet.

Around 1680 the next Guge monarch also had to repel Ladakhi invaders. After the first skirmishes, the Buddhist rulers in Leh are said to have engaged Muslim mercenaries from Kashmir in 1685 to drive out the king. In the face of this onslaught, everyone in

Tsaparang surrendered in exchange for safe passage, but they were brutally murdered all the same. From that time on the glories of Tsaparang, and with it the Guge kingdom, slowly melted into oblivion.

Yet, despite its downfall and the consequent erosion and decay, as well as the destruction of the Cultural Revolution, many ancient wonders remain to be admired.

There are three main routes to Toling, Tsaparang and the Guge kingdom. Below we describe the southern route from Lake Manasarovar into Guge and the northern route back from Guge to Darchen. There is also a third route in from Rutok and Ali in the north.

THE SOUTHERN ROUTE TO GUGE

Altitude range	4550m to 3800m
Time	9+hrs
Distance	270km
Altitude loss	750m
Highest point	5600m

Lake Manasarovar to Toling

This is a very long day if you take the southern route, but well worth it if your driver is willing, for its stunning proximity to the Indian Himalayas. The scenery along this road is quite out of this world. Make sure you are prepared with emergency food and water supplies because the route is extremely remote. The road initially passes the deep gorge on the west side of Kailash, affording another view of this mesmerising mountain.

From Lake Manasarovar, a track heads north for about 15km to join the main road near Barga. From this junction, it is about 15km west to the Darchen turnoff

Routes to Guge
(Toling and Tsaparang)
to Rutok/Ali/Kashgar
Leo Pugyal
Shipki La
Tiak
Namru
Dzo Nakpo
TIBET
Ayi La
Laoche La
Sutlej river
Dungkar
Tsaparang
Sogto
Bogo La
Toling/Zanda
Mangang
Moincer
Dawa
Tirthapuri
Kailash
Sutlej river
Dongpo
Khyunglung
Darchen
Barga
Kamet
Lake Rakhas Tal
Lake Manasarovar
INDIA
Gurla Mandhata
Nanda Devi
Purang
Trisul
Nanda Kot
Api
NEPAL
N
0 25 50 km

Nanda Devi range/ Indian Himalayas from near Khyunglung

and another 10km to the Toling road. This route leaves the main Darchen-Rutok road at about Km1325 on the milestones.

After turning south into some low hills and a wide valley, the road climbs higher and higher and the white dome of Kailash is displayed to ever greater advantage. Suddenly from the crest of a ridge the astonishing majesty of the Indian Himalayas is before your eyes – Nanda Kot, the Nanda Devi peaks, Trisul, Changabang, Panch Chuli, Kamet and the peaks of Ladakh... the list is endless.

Heading down into an eroded valley, the road snakes into a small canyon, over a higher flat-topped pass and down the hill to a river (about 40km from the turnoff). This river seems to be the true source of the Sutlej river, but it is not considered to be so. There are some very dramatic, weirdly fluted mud features to the south on the east side of this big valley. The road follows the east bank north before crossing the river on a good bridge. The river plunges into a hidden mysterious gorge ahead, and somewhere it joins the Sutlej.

The roof of the world here is dissected by innumerable deep gorges that slash through the earth, so the road must descend and re-ascend constantly to make any progress. ▸

At about 130km from the turnoff, in a tributary valley of the Sutlej, is a village with a small copper mine set below craggy cliffs of conglomerate. Three more major canyons follow. In one is a large monastery, the Dongpo Gompa. The lower structure is the main monastery, and above is a ruined fort. Further amazing scenery follows, as the route dives in and out of the contorted erosion features, sandstone spires, cathedral-like lines of pinnacles and a general disorder of ghostly turrets.

Within these gorges are endless rock formations of incredible beauty, with shapes and colours that defy imagination.

At Dawa (220km) is the monastery of the 'Valley of the Moon Castle', perched high on the rocks above the village. There are many hermit caves, ruins that are almost impossible to discern from the mudstones, and a couple of red chapels. Unfortunately there is also a checkpost here, so it may not be advisable to take too many photos.

From Dawa a rough track climbs out on to the plains. After some smaller gullies, there is another drop into a wider valley that hides the village of Mangang and the remains of a *gompa*. After another canyon with towering

Views of Mangang valley

cliffs of eroded mud stalactite and stalagmite-like features, the route finally joins the Sutlej canyon. The views remain dramatic for about another 12km to Toling, now called Zanda on modern maps.

Make sure you are carrying emergency supplies of food and water.

There is almost no traffic on this road; we saw just two trucks and one 4x4 all day. ◂ Toling was the largest and most active monastery in western Tibet and the Guge kingdom. The modern town of Zanda comprises the monastery, a Tibetan village and a smart new main street lined with Chinese shops, cafés and hotels as well as a post office and telecommunications centre. A few poplar trees shade part of the newer area.

Accommodation

Guge Hotel double/triple 80–100 Yuan per bed. Although the rooms leave much to be desired, with filthy outside toilets, the beds are good. There is no food here but there is a water tap.

Hubei Hotel One of two Chinese-style hotels (*binguans*).

Eating out

Tourist Café, or the one next door, called **Coffee Café**. The food available at the Tourist Café will tantalise your taste buds, reminding them of stimuli long forgotten.

Toling monastery

The Toling monastic complex is a walled compound entered from the east. The monastery had at least six main chapels until the Cultural Revolution began in 1966. The area now contains two substantially intact buildings. The third, known as the golden house, the Yeshe O temple, is at the heart of the complex. Built in the shape of a mandala, the temple has sadly been little restored, although work seems to be ongoing. Two other

Toling, Yeshe O mandala temple

once magnificent chapels, the Neten Lhakang and the Tongyu chapel, have been completely destroyed.

Yeshe O mandala temple

This remains as a shell, with much of the interior bleak and bare. However, the outside walls have been repainted and at each corner magnificent colourful *chortens* stand proud. The central deity was Vairocana, whose image, in wrathful and normal pose in western Tibet, was very common. There is a small museum area in the entrance chapel. A walk around the outside of the main chapel reveals a number of rooms where virtually all the shrines have been obliterated.

Lhakang Marpo

The red temple of Toling monastery is the main hall – the *dukhang*. Rinchen Zangpo probably lived here. The paintings in this dark and eerie temple are hard to see. A torch will reveal a few isolated examples of the Kashmiri art for which Guge is famous. In the back chamber the three Buddhas of past, present and future have been rebuilt. These are Dipankar, Sakyamuni and Maitreya.

Toling, Serkhang chorten

Lhakang Karpo

This is the white temple. Behind the large deodar (Indian cedar) wooden doors lies an amazing spectacle of artwork. Sadly all the statues have been wrecked. Paintings on the right walls are better preserved, with images of Tibetan deities and icons from Kagyu-pa to Gelug-pa. Entry to Toling monastery is 80 Yuan.

Serkhang chorten

An impressive monument in the northwest corner of the new Chinese garden, this has been well restored. Another *chorten*, probably consecrated by Yeshe O, is located to the southwest of the main Tibetan quarter.

High up on the tremendous craggy pinnacles above Toling town to the south are the remains of two former clifftop structures and some meditation caves. It was high above these that Lama Govinda located a chapel containing a ferocious image of the buffalo-headed demon, Dorje Jigje or Yamantaka. Professor Tucci suggests that these structures, now practically in ruins, were the summer residences of the monks. The buildings included temples, chapels with frescoes, statues, tunnels and meditation caves.

Toling to Tsaparang

Altitude range	3800m to 3850m
Time	1hr
Distance	25km
Altitude gain	50m

Tsaparang lies about 20–25km southwest of Toling. The sometimes frighteningly narrow road clings to the soft eroded crumbling hillsides above the Sutlej river and sweeps majestically into a number of side canyons, where it appears to defy gravity. This drive is sensational.

Tsaparang

In front of us the whole hillside is covered with tremendous ruins; a dead city which seems to be keeping vigil over the desolate abandonment of the yellow, tormented waste of stones, with the empty eye-sockets of its ruined castle and of its ruinous troglodytic dwellings...

Secrets of Tibet Giuseppe Tucci

Set within cliffs of fairytale sandstone organ pipes and spires, the fortress monastic complex of Tsaparang is a tremendous sight. The remnants of the city, mysterious hermit caves and ghostly mud ruins cling to the side of a dramatic hill some 100m to 150m high. Although you may puff your way up the steep hillside, you will soon forget the discomfort you have had to go through to get here.

View from Tsaparang over Sutlej valley

This hilltop fortress is home to the most exquisite murals and paintings remaining in modern Tibet. The dismembered limbs and heads of forlorn statues remain to remind us of the beauty and craftsmanship that was created so carefully 700 years ago, and destroyed so carelessly during the Cultural Revolution. No photos are allowed inside the monasteries. The main sights are listed below.

Drolma Lhakang

The first chapel is the Drolma Lhakang, also known as the Chapel of the Prefect. Paintings probably date from the 16th century. Inside are Sakyamuni, Tsong Khapa, Atisha and various bodhisattvas, as well as amazing depictions of animals, including snow lions and bird images.

Lhakang Karpo

The Lhakang Karpo or white chapel contains fabulous Kashmiri/Nepalese-style wall paintings, but most of the statues of the deities are in ruins. This chamber once housed a large Sakyamuni Buddha and at least 20 other statues. The two best-preserved statues in Tsaparang guard the entrance inside the doors. These powerful protectors are the red Tamdrin and the blue Channa Dorje. The thin, colourfully painted wooden supports were hauled across the passes from India.

Lhakang Marpo

The Lhakang Marpo is the red chapel and has some amazing artwork. The wooden carved doors are thought to be original. Inside images include Chenresig, Tara and Manjushri. On the right are the famous depictions of the life of the Buddha. Various *chortens*, still mostly intact, also grace the chamber. There are several exquisite Kashmiri miniatures featuring groups of turbaned courtiers.

Dorje Jigje Lhakang

This smaller chapel is the house of the wrathful deity, Yamantaka. It once housed a ferocious image of this

Tsaparang citadel ruins

buffalo-headed demon. There are some striking gold-painted images in this chapel. Deities displayed include Demchok, Tsong Khapa, Drolma, Maitreya and Kubera riding a snow lion.

Tsaparang Dzong or Citadel

Towering above, this complex can be reached after the ruins of the monks' quarters by an almost hidden tunnel that starts at the base of an insurmountable cliff. A couple of windows on the west side open out to give a stupefying view down the cliffs. **Take care here** as the ground is uneven and the slopes steep. Do not fall out of the windows!

Summer palace

The Summer Palace, which has been partially restored, has an amazing view over the Sutlej valley. The inside walls have been painted and a low-walled balcony offers a sunny perch once used by royalty to keep warm. The drop is sensational; this is not a place for those with vertigo. As far as the eye can see, there are weirdly eroded castle-like bands stacked one upon the other. Floating above are snow-covered mountains that eventually link into the Zanskar and Ladakh ranges.

Winter palace

The winter palace is a very cold, eerie place and might easily be missed, because the access is hidden and steep. A cable has been installed to help visitors climb down an eroding stairway. Some of the ceilings are low; you may end up crawling from room to room and tunnel to tunnel.

Demchok Lhakang

Also up here is the Demchok 'Mandala' Lhakang, a smallish red chapel with restored images on the exterior. Unfortunately this chapel was closed and undergoing repair at the time of writing. Inside the chapel there was once a three-dimensional mandala devoted to Demchok, the deity of Kailash.

Entry to Tsaparang, currently 110 Yuan, is paid for at the custodian's house close to the main entrance doorway. This fee should be included in your package on group tours.

The immediate vicinity of the Tsaparang ruins offers any number of short leg-stretchers; just head south into the jumble of canyons and maze of towers, but don't get lost! Apart from the short trek described below, there are no specific walking trails, but local tracks criss-cross the region.

A walk from Tsaparang

Altitude range	3900m to 3850m
Time	45+mins
Distance	3km
Altitude loss	50m

This is a delightful walk back to the main Toling road, following in reverse the ancient entrance route to the citadel from the Sutlej river. It can take in a visit to the Lotsang Lhakang, the *chorten* and ruined chapel seen across the small river valley to the northeast of the main complex.

From the main entrance of Tsaparang, head downhill across the rough and at times loose slopes. It can be a little tricky, since there are small gullies to be crossed. There is an indistinct route down into the small valley east of the main complex, which runs roughly towards the far hillside ruins and *chorten*. Once into the flat-bottomed small valley, take care crossing any streams. On the far side a steep track leads to the ruins (the Lotsang Lhakang chapel). ◂ The main walk proceeds down the valley, whose floor can be spongy and wet in places. It is best to stick to the east side of the valley at first. After 15mins down, it may be wiser to keep to the west side of the canyon, to avoid steeper slopes and marshy ground. Descending further, the walls of the canyon become much higher and eventually the track begins to wind around a couple of bends. After 10mins, ignore a canyon to the right and keep walking down until you reach the dusty road from Tsaparang village back to Toling.

It is worth taking this short detour for an amazing look back at Tsaparang as well as the contorted scenes of the weathered cliffs and caves.

View of Tsaparang from the valley walk

View from Tsaparang over Sutlej valley

Other hikes

Those well acclimatised and with a lot of time might consider walking from Tsaparang to Toling. In fact, with virtually no traffic, it would be exciting to do this walk, particularly the last 15km into Toling, for the eroded gullies, canyons and pinnacles are quite incredible. The side canyons 5km before Toling defy belief. Allow a full day to do this walk and remember to take plenty of water and snacks.

Other walks are possible in the Toling/Tsaparang area, but a local guide should be engaged, as it would be very easy to become disorientated in the maze of canyons, gullies and valleys. The local authorities may frown upon such activities at present, but as more tourists and travellers come to Toling, guided walks might well become more popular.

The potential for longer treks in the region is obvious. One would be the southern route from Tirthapuri to Toling via Gurugyam, the Bon citadel of Khyunglung

Ngulkar, Dongpo Gompa, Dawa and Mangang Gompas. It would take 11–12 days, and would be a classic hike through the heart of the Guge kingdom. West of Tsaparang and Toling are hidden valleys, ruined monasteries and unknown canyons with routes leading to the famous Shipki La pass into Indian Spiti, an explorer's dream destination.

The Northern Route from Guge to Darchen

Toling to Darchen

Altitude range	3800m to 4650m
Time	6–7hrs
Distance	240km
Altitude gain	850m
Highest point	5750m

For the return journey to Darchen it is possible to take a shorter alternative route, one which goes even higher. This is another day of breathtaking splendour, looking down on a foreground of contorted canyons displaying vibrant colours and shapes, with the shimmering white curtain of the Himalayas in the background.

Leaving Toling, the road heads out to the north and crosses the Sutlej river on a new bridge next to an ancient chain bridge. The route climbs and snakes its way steadily up through more eroded valleys on to a flat plain above. ◂

An unparalleled view of the Indian Himalayas extends from Ladakh to Nepal, including the gap of the Shipki pass to Indian Spiti.

Heading east, the road climbs up and around into two sheltered valleys. Nomadic Drokpa herders use this area to graze their yaks. A climb to well over 5500m brings you to a pass at 82km from Toling. The route follows an almost hidden valley, but it still continues a gradual climb. Across the distant valley are rugged multi-

coloured mountainsides, where some mining is taking place. The route also passes some amazing rocky hillsides, with varied colours of orange, red, green and yellow. Once over a steep pass at 110km, it is downhill for 11km to the main road. There is a Chinese military post here and a Tibetan teahouse, where you can stop to stretch your legs and perhaps take some limited refreshments. A milestone here indicates this as Km1215.

The main road here, coming from Rutok and Ali to Darchen, is in good shape and fast: 80kph or even more! Time permitting, it is worth a detour to Tirthapuri. The junction is at Moincer, 70km before Darchen. The turnoff for Darchen is at Km1335, a 2hr drive on the main road.

Views on the road from Toling to Darchen

RETURN TO KATHMANDU OR LHASA

The thought of the long return journey by bumpy road may seem rather daunting, but don't be put off. The scenery is just as stunning, if not even more so, when viewed from the other direction, and you may well may have different weather conditions.

When we drove west to Kailash, we narrowly escaped a heavy snowstorm, which had cut off various parts of Nepal and Tibet. The sand dunes en route were completely covered in snow, though when we reached Paryang we left the storms far behind and drove on into clear blue skies and dazzling sunshine. On our return, the skies were crystal clear and the freshly coated white peaks glimmered like diamonds in the distance.

There is always something new to see, and the notes below show the points of interest with milestone distances. (See overview map of the Himalayan region.)

Darchen to Paryang

Time	6hrs
Distance	245km

From Darchen to the Maryum La pass is 145km. The solitary lunch teahouse is 160km from Darchen. At Km1520 to the north is a massive tower-like mountain, which has the appearance of Cerro Torre in Patagonia. Paryang is close to the Km1605 milestone.

Paryang to Saga

Time	5hrs
Distance	240km

It takes about 2 hrs to reach Drongba. Km1727 is at a notable pass. Lhatsekhang village is near Km1760. Around Km1794 look out for some old fortress ruins. Km1805 is close to a dramatic monastery on the hillside

Yaks on the plains near Paryang, with the Himalayas of northwest Nepal behind

to the north. Km1823 marks a small ruined *gompa*. Km1840 is the pass before Saga, and Km1845 is Saga.

IT'S SNOW USE GOING ON

Can you get a motor vehicle over a 5000m pass when it's stuck in three feet of snow? You can try if you're Tibetan. All you need is a borrowed shovel and plenty of energy built on yak meat and *tsampa* (roasted barley).

We could hardly believe the amount of snow that had been dumped on the northern slopes of Xixapangma after the three-day storm over two weeks ago, because it was crystal clear when we got there.

For five hours we crept forward in the snow, often digging with our bare hands. We were getting rapidly out of breath, with diminishing energy levels. Too many noodles and just not enough yak meat! With the sun sinking rapidly towards the jagged skyline of Ganesh Himal, a night here was too much to contemplate. So it was back to Saga for noodles, then an 800km detour, which included a view of the North Face of Everest. Such is life behind the Himalayas!

Heavy snow on the road to Pekhu Tso

Saga to Sangsang

Time	4hrs
Distance	142km

About 1hr east of Saga and at 40km is a pass, and at Km55 you turn off north. Raka is at Km63. The scenery to the north is gaunt and stark with endless ranges of mountains, while to the south are jagged folded ranges. Much of the road is good but rough, as it hugs a narrow ledge through the Raka Tsangpo gorges. At Km2025 you reach the settlement of Sangsang. There is a guesthouse on the east side of town. It is quite cosy, but you may not want to risk the toilets at night! Namring is at Km2085 and the Lhatse junction is at Km2140.

Sangsang to Zhangmu

Time	10hrs
Distance	510km

Sangsang to Lhatse (115km) takes about 2hrs.

From Lhatse the main road heads east to Xigatse and on to Lhasa (approx 470km). This journey can be done in one very long day, now that a new direct road has opened along the Tsangpo river gorge between Xigatse and Lhasa.

Those heading back to Kathmandu have to cross a pass. After this pass, the road has now been sealed, and it should take around 3hrs to reach Xegar from Sangsang.

New Xegar (Shegar) village

Xegar (Shegar)

The modern but traditional-looking settlement of Xegar was formerly just a checkpost and scruffy mud-walled truckstop. Today travellers can revel in its pleasant local style cafés en route. For those with time, just 7km west is the ancient citadel fortress of old Shegar. The *dzong* here, known as the Shining Crystal Mountain Fortress, is a spectacular sight, clinging to the side of a jagged mountain. A further five hours' drive is needed to reach the border from Xegar, but this too should reduce significantly when the road is sealed all the way.

Accommodation

Kangjong Guesthouse, **Hotel Mount Everest View**, **Hotel Sichuan** and **Qomolungma Guesthouse**.

Eat at Kangjong, Friendship café or Amdo café.

Tingri

About two hours or less from Xegar, this traditional village commands a fabulous view across the plateau south towards the Himalayan giants. Everest, Gyachung Kang, Cho Oyu and the Rolwaling Himal rise directly from the yak-herding plains. The trek to the Rongbuk monastery/North Base Camp area at the foot of the north face of Everest sets out from here. It takes three to four days to complete and, with permits, you can continue up past the old pre-war camp that the likes of climbers Bruce, Odell, Mallory and Irvine used in the early attempts on the highest peak. Details of this trek are included in *Everest, a Trekker's Guide* (Cicerone).

Accommodation

Basic rooms can be found at the **Snow Leopard** guesthouse to the east of Tingri, or the **Snowlands** to the west.

Qomolungma National Park

The park was established in 1989. The drive to the Rongbuk monastery and Everest North Base Camp is dramatic and well worth doing if you have the time.

The turn off to the park is at about Km5145 on the main road southwest of Xegar. It takes another 3hrs to drive the 90km to Rongbuk. The main pass and viewpoint is the Pang La pass (5120m). From here the road drops down to the Dzaka valley, with a few small villages en route that have basic guesthouses and food.

At an altitude of around 5000m, the Rongbuk monastery belongs to the Nyingma-pa sect and was established around 1902. It has close links to Tengboche in the Khumbu region of Nepal. The walk to Base Camp (5200m) from here takes about 2hrs, passing first the Rongchung retreat, then the rebuilt Sherab Choling hermitage on the left.

Entry to the park is 65 Yuan per person and 400 Yuan for a car. A ride in a cart from Rongbuk monastery up to Everest North Base Camp costs 65 Yuan. You are

Everest north face from Rongbuk at sunset

not permitted to take your own vehicle up to Base Camp; from Rongbuk you must travel in a cart, or walk. Permits are required for treks above Base Camp.

From Tingri the road heads northwest and then Km5264.5 marks the turnoff to Pekhu Tso. Km5282 is where the shortcut route turns off the main road. The Lalung La pass is at Km5290 and Km5334 is the track for Milarepa's Cave. Nyalam is at Km5345 and Zhangmu is at Km5375.

Accommodation in Zhangmu

Sherpa Hotel 150 Yuan with good food.

Many other hotels, of varying degrees of sophistication and facilities.

THE LAST WORD

We turn round, as if to say farewell to the road we have travelled, as one might take leave of a dear friend; caravan life accustoms one to this love of the road. That long, weary march, that desperate attack and conquest of mountain peaks, those venturesome descents, all give one a feeling of intimate kinship with the country. We recall the various incidents, the horrors and the fascination; civilisation makes us the gift of speed but detaches us from this direct contact with nature; the motor carries us onward, almost abducts us, and the country flees from in front of us before we have been able to fix our impressions of it, vanishes swiftly, is lost like a far-off dream.

Secrets of Tibet Giuseppe Tucci

Tibet is a country perhaps like no other on earth. Though the capital city of Lhasa is now expanding rapidly, with high-rise modern buildings spreading across the plains below the magnificent Potala Palace, travelling to the remote parts of Western Tibet, as described in this book, may seem like a journey back several centuries.

In a small teahouse in the middle of nowhere, a young family with two babies provides us almost instantly with tea and noodles. Nomadic herders live in their heavy tents, moving on as the feeling takes them, or as their yaks require fresh grazing.

Apart from the mobile phone network now provided by the Chinese Army, these people live as their forefathers have done for many hundreds of years. However physically uncomfortable we may feel, it is a rare privilege to be able to visit such a land and experience the welcome that only people like the Tibetans who live in these wild mountainous lands can offer.

Tibetan village west of Tingri and Gutso

You may not enjoy the salty Tibetan butter tea, but Tibet and the land around Kailash are sure to captivate your heart and soul for the rest of your life.

APPENDIX 1

Bibliography

Allen, Charles *A Mountain in Tibet* Abacus, 1982

Allen, Charles *The Search for Shangrila* Little, Brown and Company, 1999

Batchelor, Stephen *The Tibet Guide* Wisdom Publications, 1998

Baumann, Bruno *Kristalspiegel – Pilgerreise zum heiligen Berg–Kailash* Nymphenburger, 2005

Baumer, Christoph *Tibet's Ancient Religion, Bön* Orchid Press, 2002

Buckley, Michael *Tibet: The Bradt Travel Guide* Bradt, 2006

Chan, Victor *Tibet Handbook* Moon Publications, 1994

Chandra, Lokesh *Buddhist Iconography* International Academy for Indian Culture (Pradeep Kumar Goel for Aditya Prakashan), 1991

Coleman, Graham *A Handbook of Tibetan Culture*, Random House, 1993

Dalai Lama *365 Daily Advice from the Heart* reprinted Element Books, 2004

Dalai Lama *An Introduction to Buddhism and Tantric Meditation* Paljor Publications, 1996

Dorje, Gyurme *Tibet* Footprint Handbooks, 2004

Duff, Dr J and **Gormly, Dr P**, *Pocket First Aid and Wilderness Medicine*, Cicerone, 2007

Francke, Rev AH *A History of Western Tibet* 1907 reprinted Pilgrims, 1998

Gibbons, Bob and **Pritchard-Jones**, Siân *A Trekking Guide to Southern Tibet* Pilgrims, 1993

Gibbons, Bob and **Pritchard-Jones**, Siân *Kathmandu – Valley of the Green-Eyed Yellow Idol* Pilgrims, 2004

Gibbons, Bob and **Pritchard-Jones**, Siân *Mustang – A Trekking Guide* Pilgrims, 1993

Gordon, Antoinette *The Iconography of Tibetan Lamaism* Munshiram Manoharlal, 1978

Govinda, Lama Anagarika *The Way of the White Clouds* Rider and Company, 1966

Handa, OC *Buddhist Western Himalaya* Indus Publishing, 2001

Hedin, Sven *A Conquest of Tibet* Book Faith India, reprinted 1994

Johnson, Russell and **Moran,** Kerry *Kailas: On Pilgrimage to the Sacred Mountain of Tibet* Thames & Hudson, 1989

Kalsang, Ladrang *The Guardian Deities of Tibet* Winsome Books, 2003

Kawaguchi, Ekai *Three Years in Tibet* reprinted Orchid Press, 2003

Khadro, Chagdud *P'howa Commentary* Pilgrims, 2003

Khosla, Romi *Buddhist Monasteries in the Western Himalaya* Ratna Pustak Bhandar, 1979

Kohn, Michael *The Shambhala Dictionary of Buddhism and Zen* Shambhala, 1991

Lama, Tsewang *Kailash Mandala: A Pilgrims Trekking Guide* Humla conservation and development association, 2002

Lhalungpa, Lobsang P *The Life of Milarepa* Book Faith India, 1997

Pranavananda, Swami *Kailash Manasarovar* Swami Pranavananda, 1949

Pritchard-Jones, Siân and **Gibbons**, Bob *Kailash and Guge – Land of the Tantric Mountain* Pilgrims, 2006

Pritchard-Jones, Siân and **Gibbons**, Bob *Ladakh – Land of Magical Monasteries* Pilgrims, 2006

Prophet, Elizabeth Clare *The Lost Years of Jesus* Book Faith India, 1994

Roerich, George *Tibetan Paintings* Gyan, 1997

Roerich, Nicholas *Altai Himalaya* reprinted Book Faith India, 1996

Snellgrove, David *Buddhist Himalaya* Himalayan Booksellers, 1995 (Asian edition)

Snelling, John *The Sacred Mountain* East-West Publications, 1983

Stein, RA *Tibetan Civilisation* Faber and Faber, 1972

Thurman, Robert and **Wise**, Tad *Circling the Sacred Mountain* Bantam Books, 1999

Tucci, Giuseppe *Cave of a Thousand Buddhas* Pilgrims Varanasi

Tucci, Giuseppe and **Ghersi**, E *Secrets of Tibet* Cosmo Publications, 1996 (Asian edition)

Tucci Giuseppe, *Transhimalaya* Nagel Publishers, 1973

APPENDIX 2

Glossary of Bon and Buddhist deities

SIGNIFICANT TIBETAN BON DEITIES

Within the Bon religion there are four main peaceful deities. These are the 'four transcendent lords', **Shenlha Wokar**, **Satrig Ersang**, **Sangpo Bumtri** and **Tonpa Shenrap Miwoche**. These deities, both peaceful and wrathful, are used as focal points for adherents to meditate on different aspects in order to understand the whole and reach enlightenment. This idea is used extensively in Buddhism too.

Shenlha Wokar is considered as the god of the priests, the white light that sets out a path. His definition appears to be similar to Amitabha, one of the Buddhist Dhyani Buddhas.

Satrig Ersang is the mother figure, the one with infinite wisdom. She is related to Prajnaparamita, the Buddhist deity of wisdom, and she rides on a lion.

Sangpo Bumtri is the procreator. He is said in some mythology to be accompanied by a hundred thousand male and ten thousand female procreators. The Khyung bird, the enemy of serpents, is the companion of this cosmic god.

Tonpa Shenrap Miwoche is the teacher. He is the Buddha Sakyamuni of the Bon. He holds the swastika sceptre in his right hand. Tonpa Shenrab represents the light which is victorious over the spirits of the underworld.

Kuntu Zangpo is similar to the Samantabhadra form of the primordial Adi Buddha of Buddhism. He is a manifestation of Shenlha Wokar, being the enlightened one who is unfettered by possessions. He is depicted black, together with his white female consort.

Kunzang Gyalwa Gyatso is a curious figure, for he is very similar and perhaps a precursor to the thousand-armed Avalokiteshvara, the Tibetan Chenresig deity of whom the Dalai Lamas are considered incarnates.

Welse Ngampa has nine heads and as a wrathful protector he represents 'piercing ferocity'. He crushes the enemies of Bon.

Sipai Gyalmo is an important protectress who can be related to Palden Lhamo in Buddhism. Sipai Gyalmo has 27 'daughters' or spirits who have hatched from eggs. She is called the queen of the world by Bon.

Welchen Gekho is a wrathful Bon deity who has nine heads and appears with a Khyung. He is venerated as Ku Lha Gekho, the deity found on Kailash.

Shangshung Meri is another wrathful deity, said to represent the god of the fire mountain of Shangshung. He has nine heads and also tramples into the ground the enemies of Bon.

Nyipangse, who also resides at Kailash, is the guarding deity of the *dzogchen* meditation teachings.

SIGNIFICANT TIBETAN BUDDHIST DEITIES

The **Dhyani Buddhas** are images encompassing the universe and four of them face the four cardinal directions. The Dhyani Buddhas were created from the meditation and wisdom of the Adi Buddha, the primordial Buddha. **Vairocana** is the first Dhyani Buddha and resides centrally in the *stupa* sanctum or on its east side. Vairocana is the illuminator to light the way. **Akshobhya** is the Dhyani Buddha who sits facing east. **Amitabha** is the oldest of the Dhyani Buddhas and he always faces west. (Opagme is his Tibetan name.) **Amoghasiddhi** is the Dhyani Buddha who faces north on a *stupa* or *chaitya*. Usually a serpent with seven heads stands behind him. **Ratna Sambhava** is the Dhyani Buddha who faces south; his right hand has its palm facing outwards. These are the more commonly used Sanskrit names.

The following are the main Tibetan deities. Names in brackets are the Sanskrit names.

Sakya Tukpa (Sakyamuni) is the pure image of the mortal Buddha, Gautama Siddhartha, born in Nepal. He has blue hair, a golden body and holds a bowl in his lap in most depictions.

Chenresig (Avalokiteshvara) is a popular and famous *bodhisattva*. He has renounced *nirvana*, the end of the cycle of rebirth. He embodies compassion (*karuna*) and remains on earth to counter distress and suffering. He is believed by many to be the creator of our universe. Avalokiteshvara in one aspect has a visual form with 11 heads and eyes on his hands. The Dalai Lama is considered to be his earthly representative.

Tsepame (Amitayus), an aspect of Amitabha, is the Buddha of Boundless Life, the Buddha associated with the practice and empowerment of longevity.

Namgyalma (Vijaye) is a goddess, a *bodhisattva*, who is one of the three deities of longevity. She has three heads and six arms and embodies victory and fearlessness.

Channa Dorje (Vajrapani) is a spiritual son of Buddha Akshobhya. He carries a *dorje* (*vajra*) and is a powerful wrathful protector in Tibet. He has monstrous Tantric powers and wears a snake around his neck.

Tamdrin (Hayagriva), who guards many shrines, is a wrathful emanation of Chenresig. He is seen in blood red with a small horse sticking out of his head. He wears a garland of skulls and has bird-like wings on his back.

Jampelyang (Manjushri) is the god of divine wisdom. He carries a sword to cut through ignorance. Worshipping Manjushri brings intellect and intelligence.

Dorje Jigje (Yamantaka), a wrathful emanation of Manjushri, is the 'slayer of death'. He is a Gelug-pa deity with a buffalo head.

Demchok (Chakra Sambhava) is the guardian deity of Kailash. He represents the union of bliss and emptiness when seen in *yab-yum* with his consort Dorje Phagmo (Vajra Varahi). Demchok is a Tantric meditation deity.

Drolma (Dolma), known as **Tara** in Sanskrit, is sacred to both Buddhists and Hindus. She represents the maternal aspect, symbolising fertility, purity and compassion. Tara can appear in different colours – red, green, white, gold, and, as Kali, dark blue. Each represents a different aspect of her nature. There are considered to be 21 aspects or forms of Drolma.

Palden Lhamo is a powerful Tibetan protectress who usually rides on a horse.

Jampa (Maitreya Buddha) is the future Buddha to come. He appears in a number of monasteries.

Medicine Buddha is engaged for healing the sick. He is often a blue colour and seen with four hands. In some chapels one may see eight versions of this Buddha.

Nagpo Chenpo (Mahakala) has strong links to Shiva with his trident. He often tramples on bodies or corpses. Mahakala is a wrathful Avalokiteshvara and is used for training the mind.

Tsong Khapa is known in Tibet as Je Rinpoche. He is the founder of the Gelug-pa sect.

In many Tibetan and Buddhist monasteries one might see paintings depicting four animals, one on top of the other. These are the **Four Harmonious Brothers** – the Elephant, the Monkey, the Rabbit and the Bird on top. These represent the harmony that can act as a direction for peace and removal of conflict.

The **Four Guardians** are the deities seen at the entrance to most monasteries. **Dhitarashtra** is the guardian of the east; he is white and holds a flute. **Virupaksha** guards the west; he is red, with a *stupa* in his right hand and a serpent in his left hand. **Virudhakla** is guardian of the south and holds a blue sword. **Vaishravana** is guardian of the north; he has a yellow banner in his right hand and a mongoose in his left hand, which usually is seen vomiting jewels. He is also called Jambhala.

Guru Rinpoche (Padma Sambhava) is the most famous icon of Tibetan Buddhism. He was an Indian Tantric master who went to Tibet in the 8th century to help spread the message of the religion there. He established the Nyingma-pa, the oldest sect of the red hats. His consort **Yeshe Tsogyal** wrote down his teachings in order that they could be revealed for future generations.

Milarepa, Tibet's poet saint, was an historical figure, around whom many legends have grown up. In his 'Hundred Thousand Songs' he left Tibet perhaps its greatest poetic legacy. Living as a human being, he suffered all the highs and lows of human existence before achieving realisation.

OTHER DEFINITIONS

bodhisattva a saint or disciple of Buddha who has delayed the attainment of nirvana and has remained to teach. They are found in the Mahayana path of Buddhism

Bon pre-Buddhist religion of Tibet

chaktsel gang one of the four places where pilgrims prostrate themselves before Kailash

chang home-brewed barley wine/beer, sometimes made with other grain

charnel ground sky burial site

chorten similar in shape to a small *stupa*. They do not normally contain relics and are mostly found in high Buddhist mountain country

chu river

dakini a female deity who can fly

dorje or **vajra** the thunderbolt that destroys ignorance. It is a complex figure-of-eight shaped metal object found at many temples and shrines

dukhang the main assembly hall of the monastery, where monks come to offer prayer and meditation collectively

dzogchen literally 'great perfection', a form of meditation of the Nyingma-pa and Kagyu-pa, practised to seek a 'a direct realisation of the nature of the mind'

dzong fortress or castle

gompa Tibetan name for a monastery

gonkhang a smaller chamber devoted to the protecting deities. Often dark and somewhat forbidding, this room may well house the images of Yamantaka, Mahakala and Palden Lhamo, among others

incarnation human form taken by a *lama* after a previous human life has ended

Khandroma the dakini who guards the pass east of Kailash

Kangyur the part of the Buddhist scriptures containing the teachings of Buddha Sakyamuni

khyang Asiatic wild ass

la mountain pass

lama (**guru** in Sanskrit) a religious teacher and guide, male or female. Very few monks and even fewer nuns are considered to be *lamas*

lha spirit

lhakang temple within a monastery

Losar Tibetan New Year festival

Mahayana the greater vehicle of Buddhism. Practitioners are dedicated to serving the welfare of all sentient beings, not only themselves

mandala in art, this is a circular pattern made of many colours, often a square or squares within a circle. It represents 'the divine abode of an enlightened being visualised during Tantric practices'

prayer flags cotton flags in five colours on which prayers are printed. These flutter in the wind, sending prayers direct to heaven. The different colours represent the five elements: earth, fire, air, water, and ether

prayer wheel a metal wheel engraved with Tibetan script and containing prayers. May either be large and fixed into a wall, or hand-held and spun while walking. Either way, the action of spinning the wheel activates the prayers

puja a ceremony offering prayers, usually for a specific purpose such as blessing a house

mani stone a (usually large) rock covered with engraved Buddhist mantras, sometimes painted

mani wall a long wall made of flat stones with Buddhist mantras engraved on them. It may also contain prayer wheels. You should always walk past one of these walls clockwise, with the wall on your right

shabje place of Buddha's footprint (there are three around Kailash)

Shambhala a mythical land, thought to lie north of Tibet

sky burial a form of burial where the dead body is cut up and fed to the vultures and large birds

stupa a large monument, usually with a square base, a dome on top and a pointed spire on top of that. The spire on top represents the levels towards enlightenment. A *stupa* may host the remains of a revered *lama* or teacher. In this case it is called a reliquary *stupa*, as it contains his 'relics' or bones, and sometimes precious items used by him

sutra a teaching of Sakyamuni Buddha. The Kangyur is a collection of sutras

tantra oral teachings and Buddhist scriptures forming part of the Kangyur, describing the use of mantras, mandalas and deities in meditation, and yoga for rechanelling bodily energies. Commonly associated with physical sexual methods of striving for enlightenment, the word is equally applicable to meditation methods using the energies of the mind

Tangyur the part of the Buddhist scriptures which contains Indian treatises or commentaries on the Buddha's teachings

thangka or **tangka** a religious painting, usually on silk fabric. Seen in all monasteries, hanging on the walls or pillars

torma a cake made of tsampa, butter and sugar. Used as an offering during religious ceremonies

tsampa roasted barley, the Tibetan staple food. Mixed with butter tea, it is made into a sort of porridge and eaten with the fingers

tsa-tsa small shapes made of clay, usually mixed with relics or sacred items. Often made of the ashes of deceased *lamas* and placed inside reliquary *stupas*

vajra see dorje

Vajrayana Buddhism the branch of Buddhism found in Tibet and associated with the tantras and Tantric ideas

yab-yum the depiction of two deities, male and female, in sexual union. Literally it means father-mother. The male represents compassion and the female wisdom. Deities found in this position depict not just a physical union, but the spiritual union that reaches to the pinnacle of awareness. This joining brings about a transformation of the fires and energies of passion to give everlasting long life

yidam a tutelary deity, the deity with whom a Tantric practitioner feels a special affinity or closeness, and whom he or she visualises in meditation

yogi an advanced male practitioner of Tantric meditation

yogini an advanced female practitioner of Tantric meditation

APPENDIX 3

Route summaries

TREKKING ROUTES

			page
Simikot to Purang camping			
Stage 1	Simikot to Tuling	4–5hrs	82
Stage 2	Tuling to Kermi	4+hrs	82
Stage 3	Kermi to Yangar	3–4hrs	84
Stage 4	Yangar to Muchu	4–5hrs	85
Stage 5	Muchu to Yari	7–8hrs	85
Stage 6	Yari to Sher and Purang	4–5hrs plus 2hrs	86
Stage 7	Purang to Lake Manasarovar/ Darchen by road	3–4hrs	87
Xixapangma hike			
Stage 1	Nyalam to Tara Tso	3hrs one way	93
Kailash Kora (as in text stages)			
Stage 1	Darchen to Chuku monastery	3–4hrs	111
Stage 2	Chuku monastery to Driraphuk	4–5hrs	117
plus	Kangyam Glacier day hike	3–4hrs	123
Stage 3	Driraphuk to Shabje Draktok	6–7hrs	124
Stage 4	Shabje Draktok to Zutrulphuk	3–4hrs	133
Stage 5	Zutrulphuk to Darchen	3–4hrs	137
Kailash Kora (camping)			
Stage 1	Darchen to Damding Donkhang	8hrs	111
Stage 2	Damding Donkhang to Jarok Donkhang	4hrs	117
Stage 3	Jarok Donkhang to Lham Chu valley	7hrs	124
Stage 4	Lham Chu valley to Darchen	6hrs	133
Kailash Kora (staying in local rooms)			
Stage 1	Darchen to Driraphuk monastery	9–10hrs	111
Stage 2	Driraphuk to Zutrulphuk monastery	9hrs	124
Stage 3	Zutrulphuk monastery to Darchen	4–5hrs	137

Other walks from Darchen

Day Hike	Darchen Ridge walk to viewpoint	6–7hrs return	141
Day Hike	Darchen to Serlung monastery	3–4hrs return	145
Day Hike	Darchen to Gyangdrak monastery	4–5hrs return	145
Day Hike	Darchen to Gyangdrak/Serlung return	7hrs	147
Inner Kora	Climbers only, via Serdung La pass	3–5 days	147

Lake Manasarovar (camping)

Stage 1	Chui to Hor village	8–9hrs	150
Stage 2	Hor village to Seralung monastery	3–4hrs	152
Stage 3	Seralung to Trugo monastery	7hrs	152
Stage 4	Trugo to Gossul monastery	4–5hrs	153
Stage 5	Gossul to Chui monastery	6hrs	154

Tsaparang walks

Short walk	Tsaparang Citadel to village	45mins to 1hr	173
Day hike	Tsaparang to Toling	5hrs	175

ROAD ROUTES

From Kathmandu

		page
Day 1	Kathmandu to Kodari	88
Day 2	Kodari to Nyalam	89
Day 3	Nyalam (add a day for acclimatising walk)	91
Day 4	Nyalam to Saga (add a day for acclimatisation if in doubt)	95
Day 5	Saga to Paryang	98
Day 6	Paryang to Lake Manasarovar	101
plus	Lake Manasarovar to Darchen	104
Day 7	Lake Manasarovar to Toling	162
Day 8	Toling and Tsaparang	169
Day 9	Toling to Darchen	176

To Kathmandu (direct)

Day 1	Darchen to Paryang	179
Day 2	Paryang to Saga	179
Day 3	Saga to Nyalam/Zhangmu	181
Day 4	Nyalam to Kathmandu	

To Kathmandu (via Everest Base Camp at Rongbuk)

Day 1	Darchen to Paryang	179
Day 2	Paryang to Saga	179
Day 3	Saga to Sangsang	181
Day 4	Sangsang to Xegar	181
Day 5	Xegar to Rongbuk; visit Everest Base Camp	183
Day 6	Rongbuk to Nyalam	184
Day 7	Nyalam to Kathmandu	

From Lhasa

(Add three days for acclimatisation and sightseeing in Lhasa)

Day 1	Lhasa to Gyangtse	104
Day 2	Gyangtse to Xigatse	105
Day 3	Xigatse to Saga	105
Day 4	Saga to Paryang	98
Day 5	Paryang to Lake Manasarovar or Darchen	101

To Lhasa (direct)

Day 1	Darchen to Paryang	179
Day 2	Paryang to Saga	179
Day 3	Saga to Xigatse	181
Day 4	Xigatse to Lhasa	181

APPENDIX 4

Language hints (Tibetan and Chinese phrases)

We give only some basic phrases, as most visitors will be in the company of Tibetan or Chinese guides. (Thanks to Philip Dorman for his help with the Chinese (Mandarin) phrases.)

	Tibetan	Chinese
General Phrases		
Hello	Tashi deley	Ni hao
How are you?	Kerang kusu depo yin pey?	Ni hao ma?
Very well	Nga debo yin	Wo hen hao
Thank you	Tu jey chay	Xie xie
Goodbye	Kaley shu (or Kaley pay)	Zaijian
Yes (it is)	La rey, la du	Shi
Yes (have)		You
No (it is not)	Mindu	Bu shi
No (don't have)		Meiyou
What is your name?	Kerang mingla karey re?	Ni jiao shenme mingzi?
My name is…	Nge mingla… min	Wo jiao…
Where is a restaurant?	Zakhang kappa du?	Nali you fanguan?
Where are you from?	Kerang kaney yin?	Ni cong nali lai?
Where are you going?	Kerang kappa doga?	Ni dao nali qu?
Do you understand?	Hakosong ey?	Ting dong le ma?
I do not understand	Hakomasong	Wu ting bu dong
Please speak slowly	Kaley kaley sung rognang	Qing jiang man yi dian
How much is it?	Cig la gong katsey rey?	Duo shao qian?
Do you have noodles?	Tukpa du gey?	You meiyou miantiao?
Where is a place to stay?	Nyelsa kappa yorey?	Nali you binguan?
Where is the toilet?	Sangjo kappa yorey?	Cesuo zai nali?
Where is there water?	Chu kappa yorey?	Nali you shui?
Guesthouse	Dronkhang	Fandian
Where is the trail to Toling?	Toling drosy lamka kagi rey?	Qu Toling de lu zai nali?
Please go slowly	Kaley kaley drorok nang	
(please walk slowly)	Qing zou man yi dian	
(please drive slowly)	Qing kai man yi dian	

	Tibetan	Chinese
I want to rent a yak	Nga yak cig leygo yu	Wo yao gu yi tou maoniu
OK	Digi rey	Hao
Other useful words		
who	su	shei
what	karey	shenme
where	kappa	nali
when	kadu	shenme shihou
how much	katsey	duoshao
good	yakpo	hao
cold	drankmo	leng
hot	tsapo	re
Food		
bread	paley	mian bao
rice	dreyn	mi fan
noodle soup	tukpa	tang mian
fried noodles	cho chow	miantiao
butter	mar	huangyou
eggs	gonga	ji dan
yak meat	nya sha	rou (meat) niu rou (beef)
beans	drayma	dou
sugar	jema kara	tang
salt	tsa	yan
water	chu	shui
boiled water	chu kolma	kaishui
black tea	ja dang	hong cha
Tibetan tea	Bhu ja	naicha (milk tea)
flask of hot water	chadam chu tsapo	reshuiping

Numbers

	Tibetan	Chinese
0	lekor	ling
1	chig	yi
2	nyi	er
3	sum	san
4	shi	si
5	nga	wu
6	druk	liu
7	dun	qi
8	gye	ba
9	gu	jiu
10	chu	shi
11	chu chig	shiyi
15	chu nga	shiwu
20	nyi chu	ershi
30	sum chu	sanshi
40	ship chu	sishi
50	ngap chu	wushi
100	gya tamba	yi bai

APPENDIX 5

Films and music

Films

Look out for *Seven Years in Tibet,* the story of Eiger summiteer Heinrich Harrer's life as a fugitive during the Second World War and his life in Lhasa close to the Dalai Lama. *Kundun* is a more esoteric look at the life of the Dalai Lama in Lhasa before 1959. *Cry of the Snow Lion* is a very sad film about Tibet. Another film shot clandestinely in Tibet is *Windhorse*. Finally, a wonderfully evocative film about the people of Dolpo in Nepal is *Himalaya,* which portrays the life of traditional village yak herders in the remote Tibetan regions.

Music

There are a lot of new CDs with Tibetan themes. A few are folksongs, but most are amalgams of Tibetan chants, songs and 'western oriental'. Surprisingly, these mixed tunes resonate with some beautiful and meditatively warming music. Some of our personal favourites are *Tibetiya, Sacred Buddha, Karmapa: Secrets of the Crystal Mountain, Tibet Impressions, Journey to Tibet, Sacred Chants of Buddha, Tibetan Incantations* and *Themes from the film Himalaya*. All these can be found in Kathmandu for 200–400 Nepalese Rupees.

APPENDIX 6

Useful addresses/websites

Tour operators in the UK

Classic Journeys 33 High Street, Tibshelf, Alfreton, Derbyshire DE55 5NX; tel: 01773 873497; www.classicjourneys.co.uk

Exodus Grange Mills, Weir Road, London SW12 0NE; tel: 020 8673 0859 or 0879 240 5550; sales@exodus.co.uk; www.exodus.co.uk

Expedition World Hollycroft Farm, Colworth, Chichester, West Sussex PO20 2DU; tel: 01243 789264; sianpj@hotmail.com; www.expeditionworld.com. A small specialist company run by the authors of this book.

Himalayan Kingdoms Old Crown House, 18 Market Street, Wotton-Under-Edge, Gloucestershire GL12 7AE; tel: 01453 844400; info@himalayankingdoms.com; www.himalayankingdoms.com

KE Adventure Travel 32 Lake Road, Keswick, Cumbria CA12 5DQ; tel: 017687 73966; info@keadventure.co.uk; www.keadventure.com

Peregrine tel: 01635 872300; www.peregrineadventures.co.uk

Trans Himalaya 16 Skye Crescent, Crieff, Perth & Kimross PH7 3FB; tel: 01764 60604; info@trans-himalaya.com; www.trans-himalaya.com. Run by Dr Gyurme Dorje, a Tibetologist and writer, this company also has an office in Chengdu, China.

Tour operators in Nepal

Ama Dablam Adventures himalaya.sales@amadablam.wlink.com.np

Sherpa Adventure Travel sat@wlink.com.np

Explore Nepal Richa Tours & Travel explore@enrtt.mos.com.np

Himalayan Encounters in the Kathmandu Guest House courtyard; himenco@wlink.com.np

Samjhana Travels also at the Kathmandu Guest House; info@ktmgh.com

Tour operators in Lhasa and Chengdu

Tibet Holyland Adventures tel: 0891 683 6652; holyland@public.ls.xz.cn

Tibet International Sports Travel tel: 0891 633 4082; tist@public.ls.xz.cn

Tibet Yungdru Adventure tel: 0891 633 6642; tny@public.ls.xz.cn

Windhorse Travel tel: 0891 683 3009; jampa_w@hotmail.com

Access Tibet Tour Jason Yang, Room 178–188, 4F Yuanheng Trade Building, #235 Shuhan Road, Chengdu 610036 China; sales@accesstibettour.net

Other websites

China Travel Service www.chinatravel.co.uk

Chinese information www.tibet.ca (Canadian site), www.tibetinfo.com/en

Downloadable maps www.tibetmap.com

Everest/Qomolungma National Park information available at qcp@mountain.org

Khampa caravan (Zhongdian to Lhasa) www.khampacaravan.com

Tibetan Government in Exile www.tibet.com

Tibet Travel Expert www.tibet-tour.com

Other Chinese embassies

Canada www.chinaembassycanada.org

Denmark www.chinaembassy.dk

France www.amb-chine.fr

Japan www.china-embassy.or.jp

New Zealand www.chinaembassy.org.nz

South Africa www.chinese-embassy.org.za

Switzerland www.china-embassy.ch

NOTES

LISTING OF CICERONE GUIDES

BACKPACKING

The End to End Trail
Three Peaks, Ten Tors
Backpacker's Britain Vol 1 – Northern England
Backpacker's Britain Vol 2 – Wales
Backpacker's Britain Vol 3 – Northern Scotland
The Book of the Bivvy

NORTHERN ENGLAND LONG-DISTANCE TRAILS

The Dales Way
The Reiver's Way
The Alternative Coast to Coast
A Northern Coast to Coast Walk
The Pennine Way
Hadrian's Wall Path
The Teesdale Way

FOR COLLECTORS OF SUMMITS

The Relative Hills of Britain
Mts England & Wales Vol 2 – England
Mts England & Wales Vol 1 – Wales

UK GENERAL

The National Trails

BRITISH CYCLE GUIDES

The Cumbria Cycle Way
Lands End to John O'Groats – Cycle Guide
Rural Rides No.1 – West Surrey
Rural Rides No.2 – East Surrey
South Lakeland Cycle Rides
Border Country Cycle Routes
Lancashire Cycle Way

CANOE GUIDES

Canoeist's Guide to the North-East

LAKE DISTRICT AND MORECAMBE BAY

Coniston Copper Mines
Scrambles in the Lake District (North)
Scrambles in the Lake District (South)
Walks in Silverdale and Arnside AONB
Short Walks in Lakeland 1 – South
Short Walks in Lakeland 2 – North
Short Walks in Lakeland 3 – West
The Tarns of Lakeland Vol 1 – West
The Tarns of Lakeland Vol 2 – East
The Cumbria Way & Allerdale Ramble
Lake District Winter Climbs
Roads and Tracks of the Lake District
The Lake District Angler's Guide
Rocky Rambler's Wild Walks
An Atlas of the English Lakes
Tour of the Lake District
The Cumbria Coastal Way

NORTH-WEST ENGLAND

Walker's Guide to the Lancaster Canal
Family Walks in the Forest Of Bowland
Walks in Ribble Country
Historic Walks in Cheshire
Walking in Lancashire
Walks in Lancashire Witch Country
The Ribble Way

THE ISLE OF MAN

Walking on the Isle of Man
The Isle of Man Coastal Path

PENNINES AND NORTH-EAST ENGLAND

Walks in the Yorkshire Dales
Walks on the North York Moors, books 1 and 2
Walking in the South Pennines
Walking in the North Pennines
Walking in the Wolds
Waterfall Walks – Teesdale and High Pennines
Walking in County Durham
Yorkshire Dales Angler's Guide
Walks in Dales Country
Historic Walks in North Yorkshire
South Pennine Walks
Walking in Northumberland
Cleveland Way and Yorkshire Wolds Way
The North York Moors

DERBYSHIRE, PEAK DISTRICT, EAST MIDLANDS

High Peak Walks
White Peak Walks Northern Dales
White Peak Walks Southern Dales
Star Family Walks Peak District & South Yorkshire
Walking In Peakland
Historic Walks in Derbyshire

WALES AND WELSH BORDERS

Ascent of Snowdon
Welsh Winter Climbs
Hillwalking in Wales – Vol 1
Hillwalking in Wales – Vol 2
Scrambles in Snowdonia
Hillwalking in Snowdonia
The Ridges of Snowdonia
Hereford & the Wye Valley
Walking Offa's Dyke Path
Lleyn Peninsula Coastal Path
Anglesey Coast Walks
The Shropshire Way
Spirit Paths of Wales
Glyndwr's Way
The Pembrokeshire Coastal Path
Walking in Pembrokeshire
The Shropshire Hills – A Walker's Guide

MIDLANDS

The Cotswold Way
The Grand Union Canal Walk
Walking in Warwickshire
Walking in Worcestershire
Walking in Staffordshire
Heart of England Walks

SOUTHERN ENGLAND

Exmoor & the Quantocks
Walking in the Chilterns
Walking in Kent
Two Moors Way
Walking in Dorset
A Walker's Guide to the Isle of Wight
Walking in Somerset
The Thames Path
Channel Island Walks
Walking in Buckinghamshire
The Isles of Scilly
Walking in Hampshire
Walking in Bedfordshire
The Lea Valley Walk
Walking in Berkshire
The Definitive Guide to Walking in London
The Greater Ridgeway
Walking on Dartmoor
The South West Coast Path
Walking in Sussex
The North Downs Way
The South Downs Way

SCOTLAND

Scottish Glens 1 – Cairngorm Glens
Scottish Glens 2 – Atholl Glens
Scottish Glens 3 – Glens of Rannoch
Scottish Glens 4 – Glens of Trossach
Scottish Glens 5 – Glens of Argyll
Scottish Glens 6 – The Great Glen
Scottish Glens 7 – The Angus Glens
Scottish Glens 8 – Knoydart to Morvern
Scottish Glens 9 – The Glens of Ross-shire
The Island of Rhum
Torridon – A Walker's Guide
Walking the Galloway Hills
Border Pubs & Inns – A Walkers' Guide
Scrambles in Lochaber
Walking in the Hebrides
Central Highlands: 6 Long Distance Walks
Walking in the Isle of Arran
Walking in the Lowther Hills
North to the Cape
The Border Country – A Walker's Guide
Winter Climbs – Cairngorms
The Speyside Way
Winter Climbs – Ben Nevis & Glencoe
The Isle of Skye, A Walker's Guide
The West Highland Way
Scotland's Far North
Walking the Munros Vol 1 – Southern, Central
Walking the Munros Vol 2 – Northern & Cairngorms
Scotland's Far West
Walking in the Cairngorms

Walking in the Ochils, Campsie Fells and Lomond Hills
Scotland's Mountain Ridges
The Great Glen Way
The Pentland Hills: A Walker's Guide
The Southern Upland Way
Ben Nevis and Glen Coe

IRELAND

The Mountains of Ireland
Irish Coastal Walks
The Irish Coast to Coast

INTERNATIONAL CYCLE GUIDES

The Way of St James – Le Puy to Santiago cyclist's guide
The Danube Cycle Way
Cycle Tours in Spain
Cycling the River Loire – The Way of St Martin
Cycle Touring in France
Cycling in the French Alps

WALKING AND TREKKING IN THE ALPS

Tour of Monte Rosa
Walking in the Alps (all Alpine areas)
100 Hut Walks in the Alps
Chamonix to Zermatt
Tour of Mont Blanc
Alpine Ski Mountaineering Vol 1 Western Alps
Alpine Ski Mountaineering Vol 2 Eastern Alps
Snowshoeing: Techniques and Routes in the Western Alps
Alpine Points of View
Tour of the Matterhorn
Across the Eastern Alps: E5

FRANCE, BELGIUM AND LUXEMBOURG

RLS (Robert Louis Stevenson) Trail
Walks in Volcano Country
French Rock
Walking the French Gorges
Rock Climbs Belgium & Luxembourg
Tour of the Oisans: GR54
Walking in the Tarentaise and Beaufortain Alps
Walking in the Haute Savoie, vol. 1
Walking in the Haute Savoie, vol. 2
Tour of the Vanoise
GR20 Corsica – The High Level Route
The Ecrins National Park
Walking the French Alps: GR5
Walking in the Cevennes
Vanoise Ski Touring
Walking in Provence
Walking on Corsica
Mont Blanc Walks
Walking in the Cathar region of south west France
Walking in the Dordogne
Trekking in the Vosges and Jura
The Cathar Way

PYRENEES AND FRANCE / SPAIN

Rock Climbs in the Pyrenees
Walks & Climbs in the Pyrenees
The GR10 Trail: Through the French Pyrenees
The Way of St James – Le Puy to the Pyrenees
The Way of St James – Pyrenees-Santiago-Finisterre
Through the Spanish Pyrenees GR11
The Pyrenees – World's Mountain Range Guide
The Pyrenean Haute Route
The Mountains of Andorra

SPAIN AND PORTUGAL

Picos de Europa – Walks & Climbs
The Mountains of Central Spain
Walking in Mallorca
Costa Blanca Walks Vol 1
Costa Blanca Walks Vol 2
Walking in Madeira
Via de la Plata (Seville To Santiago)
Walking in the Cordillera Cantabrica
Walking in the Canary Islands 1 West
Walking in the Canary Islands 2 East
Walking in the Sierra Nevada
Walking in the Algarve
Trekking in Andalucia

SWITZERLAND

Walking in Ticino, Switzerland
Central Switzerland – A Walker's Guide
The Bernese Alps
Walking in the Valais
Alpine Pass Route
Walks in the Engadine, Switzerland
Tour of the Jungfrau Region

GERMANY AND AUSTRIA

Klettersteig Scrambles in Northern Limestone Alps
King Ludwig Way
Walking in the Salzkammergut
Walking in the Harz Mountains
Germany's Romantic Road
Mountain Walking in Austria
Walking the River Rhine Trail
Trekking in the Stubai Alps
Trekking in the Zillertal Alps
Walking in the Bavarian Alps

SCANDINAVIA

Walking In Norway
The Pilgrim Road to Nidaros (St Olav's Way)

EASTERN EUROPE

The High Tatras
The Mountains of Romania
Walking in Hungary
The Mountains of Montenegro

CROATIA AND SLOVENIA

Walks in the Julian Alps
Walking in Croatia

ITALY

Italian Rock
Walking in the Central Italian Alps
Central Apennines of Italy
Walking in Italy's Gran Paradiso
Long Distance Walks in Italy's Gran Paradiso
Walking in Sicily
Shorter Walks in the Dolomites
Treks in the Dolomites
Via Ferratas of the Italian Dolomites Vol 1
Via Ferratas of the Italian Dolomites Vol 2
Walking in the Dolomites
Walking in Tuscany
Trekking in the Apennines
Through the Italian Alps: the GTA

OTHER MEDITERRANEAN COUNTRIES

The Mountains of Greece
Climbs & Treks in the Ala Dag (Turkey)
The Mountains of Turkey
Treks & Climbs Wadi Rum, Jordan
Jordan – Walks, Treks, Caves etc.
Crete – The White Mountains
Walking in Western Crete
Walking in Malta

AFRICA

Climbing in the Moroccan Anti-Atlas
Trekking in the Atlas Mountains
Kilimanjaro

NORTH AMERICA

The Grand Canyon & American South West
Walking in British Columbia
The John Muir Trail

SOUTH AMERICA

Aconcagua

HIMALAYAS – NEPAL, INDIA

Langtang, Gosainkund & Helambu: A Trekkers' Guide
Garhwal & Kumaon – A Trekkers' Guide
Kangchenjunga – A Trekkers' Guide
Manaslu – A Trekkers' Guide
Everest – A Trekkers' Guide
Annapurna – A Trekker's Guide
Bhutan – A Trekker's Guide
The Mount Kailash Trek

TECHNIQUES AND EDUCATION

The Adventure Alternative
Rope Techniques
Snow & Ice Techniques
Mountain Weather
Beyond Adventure
The Hillwalker's Manual
Outdoor Photography
The Hillwalker's Guide to Mountaineering
Map and Compass
Sports Climbing Handbook
An Introduction to Rock Climbing

MINI GUIDES

Avalanche!
Snow
Pocket First Aid and Wilderness Medicine
Navigation

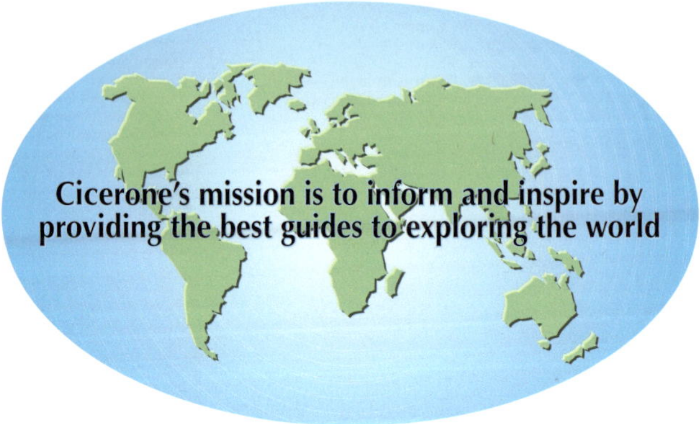

Since its foundation over 30 years ago, Cicerone has specialised in publishing guidebooks and has built a reputation for quality and reliability. It now publishes nearly 300 guides to the major destinations for outdoor enthusiasts, including Europe, UK and the rest of the world.

Written by leading and committed specialists, Cicerone guides are recognised as the most authoritative. They are full of information, maps and illustrations so that the user can plan and complete a successful and safe trip or expedition – be it a long face climb, a walk over Lakeland fells, an alpine traverse, a Himalayan trek or a ramble in the countryside.

With a thorough introduction to assist planning, clear diagrams, maps and colour photographs to illustrate the terrain and route, and accurate and detailed text, Cicerone guides are designed for ease of use and access to the information.

If the facts on the ground change, or there is any aspect of a guide that you think we can improve, we are always delighted to hear from you.

Cicerone Press
2 Police Square Milnthorpe Cumbria LA7 7PY
Tel:01539 562 069 Fax:01539 563 417
e-mail:info@cicerone.co.uk web:www.cicerone.co.uk

CICERONE